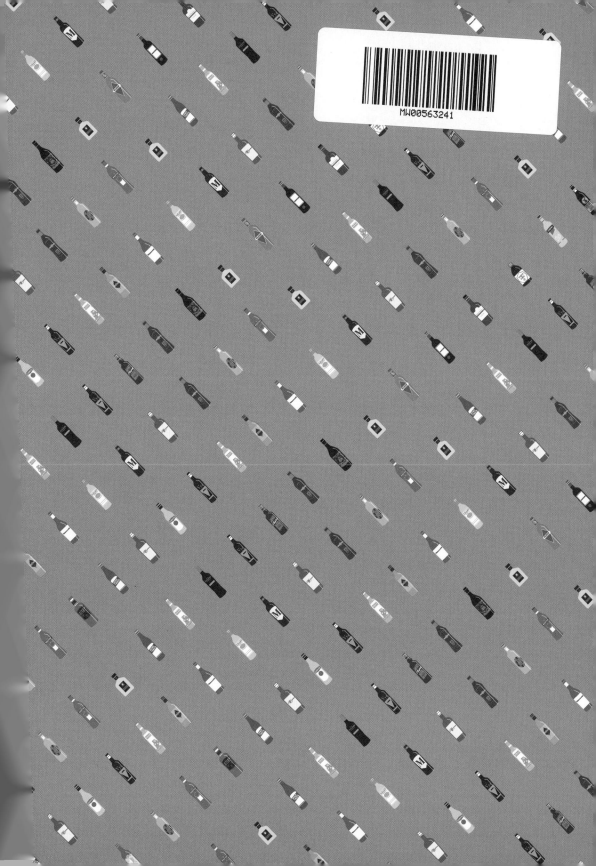

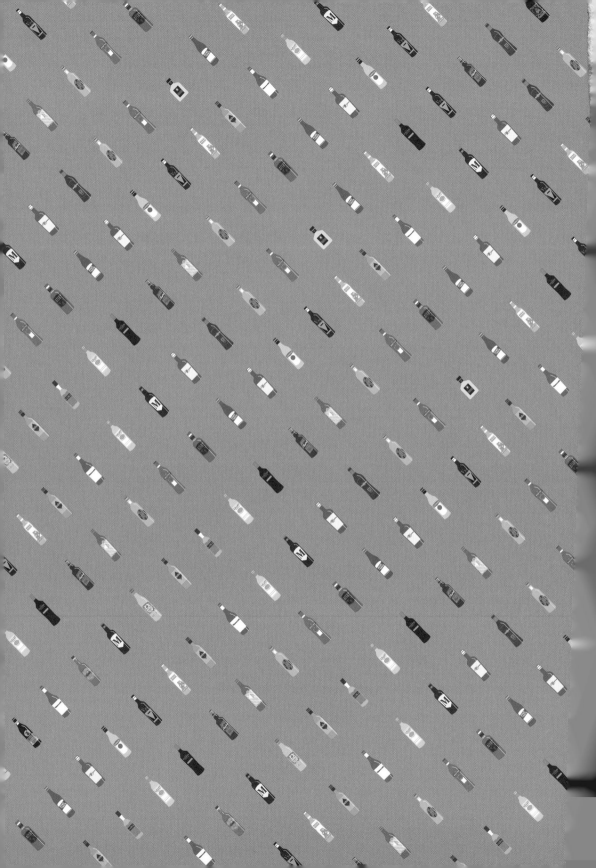

THE BOOK OF

VERMOUTH

A BARTENDER AND A WINEMAKER
CELEBRATE THE WORLD'S GREATEST APERITIF

SHAUN BYRNE & GILLES LAPALUS

hardie grant books

KEY

GILLES LAPALUS THE WINEMAKER

SHAUN BYRNE THE BARTENDER

JUDE MYALL THE BOTANIST

TIM ENTWISLE THE BOTANIST

CAMERON MACKENZIE THE DISTILLER

CONTENTS

FROM THE WINEMAKER

Vermouth is mainly familiar to a young generation in cocktail bar circles, and, indeed, to a generation of drinkers who are well into their retirement.

But, more recently, it has been making waves in the media and appearing on restaurant tables. The name is familiar to many, thanks to the reach of some global brands, but the average drinker will rarely consider vermouth a wine. Used mostly with spirits, it is often cited in the 'spirit' category.

'What is vermouth?' is usually the first question I am asked when I begin a conversation about it. Having been in the wine industry for most of my life, I approach vermouth from a wine angle. As you will discover in the Production chapter (see page 34), vermouth is, after all, mainly wine. Or, more precisely, an aromatised wine.

I have also approached vermouth from a historical perspective. This arose from my exploration of how Benedictine monks at the Abbey of Cluny made hippocras, a medieval aromatised wine. In this section, you'll discover that vermouth has a long history. It reaches as far back as that of wine itself, which makes its evolution truly fascinating and a dynamic expression of the times.

The history of this beverage leads us into the world of botanicals – the very ingredients that inform a vermouth's flavour.

From the first archaeological discoveries, to the Spice Routes and Indigenous Australians' use of native plants, there is an infinite world to explore, illustrated by the variety of vermouths available and multiple ways of producing this aromatised wine.

A second question often arrives quickly after I give the definition of vermouth: 'How do you use it?'. Instantly, my winemaker brain suggests it complements food, or you drink it neat, even though it was my discovery of the Negroni that lured me to the production of one of its vital ingredients. It is such a privilege to have so many great chefs currently embracing the use of vermouth, either in a dish or paired with one. Inevitably, though, I am an advocate for treating vermouth as you would wine: served with a meal. Accompanied by some of the best bartenders in the world, Shaun, the bartending expert and my business partner in Maidenii, will explore the universe of mixing drinks with vermouth.

It has been fascinating to discover this versatile drink, especially in comparison to wine. Wine is sacred, and the language and, especially, the handling of wine – from the cellar, to the service and even the glass – is highly ceremonial, its veneration suggesting it should be left unadulterated. Similarly, vermouth can shine when drunk on its own, but it also finds its home in mixed drinks. In the same way a chef selects the best-quality ingredients to create a dish, so too can a fine vermouth help to form a beautiful cocktail.

Finally, a recurring sticking point is that abandoned bottle of vermouth. Often a bottle can be found left open for months or years at a time in a cupboard or on a bar shelf. I hope this book invites you to find a use for that forgotten bottle and, more importantly, gives you plenty of ideas for making vermouth a permanent part of your repertoire.

Santé!

– GILLES LAPALUS

FROM THE BARTENDER

A lot of people ask me how I came to start producing vermouth.

The story goes that I was working at Gin Palace and trying to make better versions of cocktail syrups than could be purchased. But I didn't just stop at syrups; I also tried my hand at making shrubs and bitters before I moved on to vermouth. I knew the basic building blocks of vermouth – wine, spirit, sugar, wormwood and other botanicals – so I sourced some ingredients and started experimenting. Initially, the results were not great, but were good enough to warrant further exploration. Knowing that vermouth is mostly wine, it seemed imperative that I seek the advice of a good winemaker, and so it was that Gilles and I met for lunch and discussed our passion for vermouth and how we could go about making it.

Vermouth and cocktails go hand in hand. They have done for years and will do for years to come. The main reason is that vermouth is so full of flavour; it has sweet, sour, bitter and even salty notes depending on the brand. This flavour spectrum makes it incredibly versatile to use, and helps emphasise different characteristics in the products it is mixed with. Historically, vermouth played second fiddle to the main spirit in a cocktail, but, due to the recent trend towards lower-alcohol drinks, vermouth has come into its own. Given its low alcohol content and full flavour, vermouth is being used more now than ever before. And there has been an explosion of brands in response to this popularity, giving bartenders a greater variety of vermouths to use in their cocktails. This is great news, as bartenders are in the ideal position to promote a product to the general population.

Educating people about vermouth, how to drink it, how to store it and how to mix it is something I am very passionate about. For many years vermouth had fallen out of favour, so much so that people had forgotten all about it. Working at Gin Palace, I would often hear people say things like 'Vermouth? That's what my grandmother drank when she was young!' Luckily, with bartenders showcasing it in cocktails, winemakers promoting it as a drink to be served neat, and people writing books on the subject, the world of vermouth has never been so exciting. So, I encourage you to grab a bottle of your favourite vermouth and drink it neat while reading Part 1 of this book, then use the rest to whip up some cocktails in Part 2.

Cheers!

– SHAUN BYRNE

vermouth essentials

HISTORY

Vermouth's history is closely associated with winemaking.

Thanks to Patrick McGovern, known as the Indiana Jones of ancient ales, wines and extreme beverages in his role as Scientific Director of the Biomolecular Archaeology Project for Cuisine, Fermented Beverages and Health at the University of Pennsylvania Museum in Philadelphia, new horizons in the history of wine are being discovered.

Over the past 15 years, new ways of analysing archaeological remains have uncovered some interesting revelations. The latest, in November 2017, was the chemical analysis of ancient organic compounds found in pottery fabrics from sites in Georgia, dating back to the early Neolithic period (ca. 6,000–5,000 BC). The results provided the earliest biomolecular archaeological evidence of grape wine and viniculture from the Near East.

In 2004, McGovern and his team discovered some remains dating back to ca. 7,000 BC in China at the Neolithic site of Jiahu in the Yellow River valley. It is possibly the earliest evidence of an alcoholic beverage, which may have been used medicinally, anywhere in the world. At a more recent site (ca. 1,050 BC), botanicals found included two aromatic compounds, most likely from a tree resin, a daisy flower or wormwood (specifically *Artemisia annua* or *Artemisia argyi*). The plants had been soaked in rice wine, which indicates the presence of the early ancestor of vermouth. To this day, these plants are still used in Chinese medicine.

In Tasmania, the sap of the cider gum tree, *Eucalyptus gunnii*, was collected to produce an alcoholic drink called *wayatinah*. In south-west Western Australia, the Noongar people steeped nectar-rich banksia flowers in water to produce a drink called *mangaitch*. In parts of south-west Queensland, an aromatised mead was made by combining bauhinia blossoms with sugarbag, a native honey.

The history of wine, and vermouth in particular, is still evolving as new discoveries add to our knowledge, but it can be broadly broken down into three eras.

THE ANTIQUE ERA

9000 BC–1500 AD, CHINA & EUROPE

During this period, wine was often mixed with other substances, particularly botanicals. The art of distillation hadn't yet been discovered and alcohol was mostly derived from the fermentation of fruits or grains. Antique-era wine was mainly used for spiritual ceremonies and, increasingly, for medicinal purposes. Notably, the Greeks used wine during symposia, while the Romans were known to have consumed wine in large quantities, signalling the consumption of wine for pleasure, not just for medicinal use. Gradually, a second era began to emerge.

THE INDUSTRIAL ERA

1500–1990 AD, MAINLY EUROPE

Until the Renaissance, aromatised wine was mainly used for medicinal purposes and the entertainment of the elite. Following the discovery of the Americas and, later, the emergence of the bourgeoisie, wine was consumed purely for pleasure. In Italy, the development of the vermouth industry began in the late eighteenth century in the alpine city of Torino. From there, an important

export industry developed to satisfy the local and new international market for vermouth. France was the second-largest player of this era, with strong export sales of vermouth, particularly to America, where the rise of the aperitif made it a direct competitor with wine. In the late nineteenth century in Spain, sherry was produced in Jerez, and *vermut* in the rest of the country, and the two products competed with each other.

THE CONTEMPORARY ERA

1990–PRESENT DAY, GLOBAL

Over the past two decades, we have witnessed a resurgence of vermouth and other aromatised aperitifs from traditional producers. New vermouths have emerged from producers in Germany, the Netherlands, the United States, New Zealand and Australia, and have been regenerated in South Africa. This revival is riding the cocktail and culinary coat-tails of boutique, crafted spirits – particularly gin – that are popular today. *L'hora del vermut*, or 'the vermouth hour', in Spain, which once fell on a Sunday after church in the local bar has now moved to the tapas or pintxos bar. The aperitivo in Italy embraced the use of bitters and, now, so too has the rest of the world. Should China produce vermouth, the geographical circle would be complete.

One significant influence of the Contemporary era is that people are consciously choosing to use and consume what is produced in their local area. In Australia, this has led to the rediscovery of native botanicals, as much in people's kitchens as in the beverage industry. In a way, this is a return to traditional principles.

ANTIQUE ERA

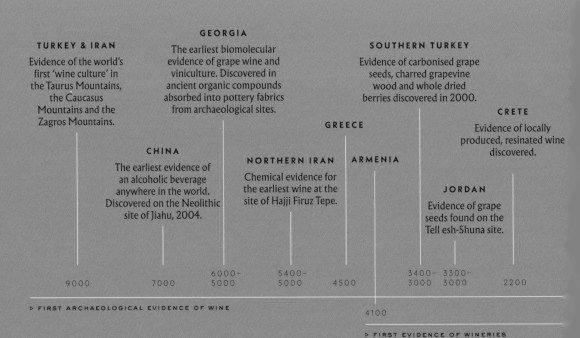

GEORGIA
The earliest biomolecular evidence of grape wine and viniculture. Discovered in ancient organic compounds absorbed into pottery fabrics from archaeological sites.

TURKEY & IRAN
Evidence of the world's first 'wine culture' in the Taurus Mountains, the Caucasus Mountains and the Zagros Mountains.

SOUTHERN TURKEY
Evidence of carbonised grape seeds, charred grapevine wood and whole dried berries discovered in 2000.

CRETE
Evidence of locally produced, resinated wine discovered.

GREECE

CHINA
The earliest evidence of an alcoholic beverage anywhere in the world. Discovered on the Neolithic site of Jiahu, 2004.

NORTHERN IRAN
Chemical evidence for the earliest wine at the site of Hajji Firuz Tepe.

ARMENIA

JORDAN
Evidence of grape seeds found on the Tell esh-Shuna site.

| 9000 | 7000 | 6000–5000 | 5400–5000 | 4500 | 3400–3000 | 3300–3000 | 2200 |

▷ FIRST ARCHAEOLOGICAL EVIDENCE OF WINE

4100

▷ FIRST EVIDENCE OF WINERIES

EGYPT
Amphore containing botanical extracts found in the tomb of an early pharaoh, Scorpion.

3100–2900

─────────────────────────────── + ─────────────────────────── **AD**

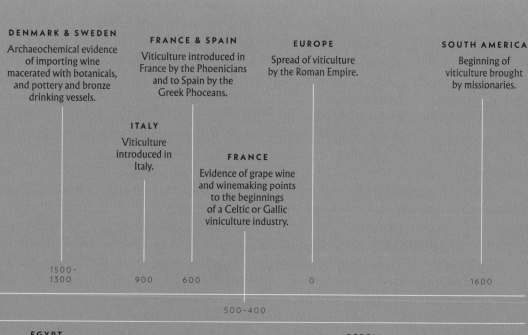

DENMARK & SWEDEN

Archaeochemical evidence of importing wine macerated with botanicals, and pottery and bronze drinking vessels.

FRANCE & SPAIN

Viticulture introduced in France by the Phoenicians and to Spain by the Greek Phoceans.

EUROPE

Spread of viticulture by the Roman Empire.

SOUTH AMERICA

Beginning of viticulture brought by missionaries.

ITALY

Viticulture introduced in Italy.

FRANCE

Evidence of grape wine and winemaking points to the beginnings of a Celtic or Gallic viniculture industry.

1500– 1300   900   600   0   1600

500–400

EGYPT

Papyri dating back to the mid-twelfth Dynasty show that 'medicinal wines' were very important to the Egyptian 'physician'.

PERSIA

Al-Razi perfects the art of distillation.

GERMANY

Liber de arte distillandi de simplicibus, Hieronymus Brunschwig.

FRANCE

Liber de Vinis, Arnaud de Villeneuve.

CHINA

Evidence of wine used in medicine is recorded in the oracle bone inscriptions of the late Shang Dynasty.

GREECE

Documented by Hippocrates.

GREECE

Claudius Galen first attempts distillation.

SPAIN

First mention of the word 'alcohol', by Ramon Llull.

ENGLAND

The Art of Distillation, John French.

1850   1200– 1046   400   129–216   865– 925   1240– 1311   1310   1450– 1512   1651

> FIRST DOCUMENTATION OF WINE & DISTILLATES

INDUSTRIAL ERA

1700 —————————— 1800 ——————————————————

Cinzano moves
to Torino to
start vermouth
production.

St Raphael
begins
production.

Joseph Noilly
creates what
will become
Noilly Prat.

Joseph
Chavasse
creates his
own *vermout*
in Chambery.
It would
eventually
become Dolin.

Cora begins
production
and export of
vermouth.

Gancia is
founded.

1700

Beginning of viticulture in North
America in the early seventeenth
century.

1763

Rise of the wealthy bourgeoisie in Italy
sees the first cafe opening in Torino, and
the first sign of the 'aperitivo hour'.

1786

Antonio Benedetto Carpano invents
his *vermut* recipe in Torino.

1750–1800

Beginning of viticulture in South
Africa in the mid-seventeenth century,
and Australia in the late seventeenth
century.

'13   '15   '21   '30   '38   '50

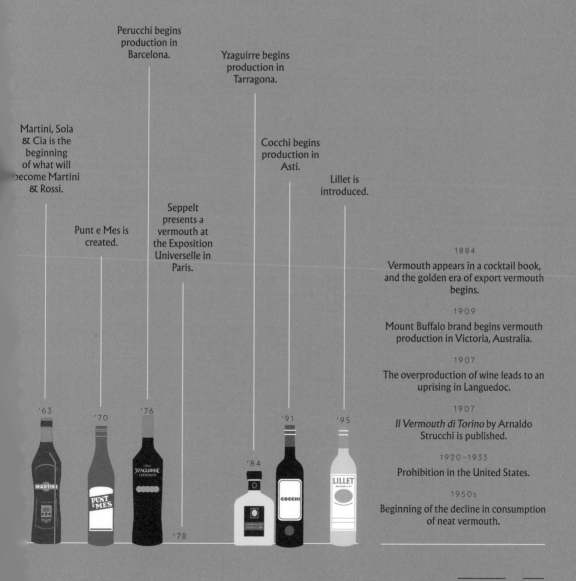

Perucchi begins
production in
Barcelona.

Yzaguirre begins
production in
Tarragona.

Martini, Sola
& Cia is the
beginning
of what will
become Martini
& Rossi.

Cocchi begins
production in
Asti.

Lillet is
introduced.

Punt e Mes is
created.

Seppelt
presents a
vermouth at
the Exposition
Universelle in
Paris.

'63   '70   '76

'91   '95

'84

'78

1884
Vermouth appears in a cocktail book,
and the golden era of export vermouth
begins.

1909
Mount Buffalo brand begins vermouth
production in Victoria, Australia.

1907
The overproduction of wine leads to an
uprising in Languedoc.

1907
Il Vermouth di Torino by Arnaldo
Strucchi is published.

1920–1933
Prohibition in the United States.

1950s
Beginning of the decline in consumption
of neat vermouth.

CONTEMPORARY ERA

1970 ——————————————— 2000 ——

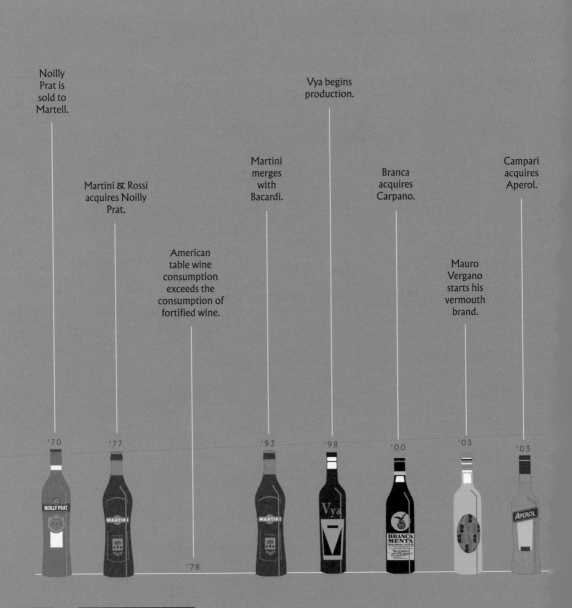

Noilly Prat is sold to Martell.

Vya begins production.

Martini & Rossi acquires Noilly Prat.

Martini merges with Bacardi.

Branca acquires Carpano.

Campari acquires Aperol.

American table wine consumption exceeds the consumption of fortified wine.

Mauro Vergano starts his vermouth brand.

'70   '77   '93   '98   '00   '03   '03

'78

NOILLY PRAT

MARTINI

MARTINI

Vya

BRANCA MENTA

APEROL

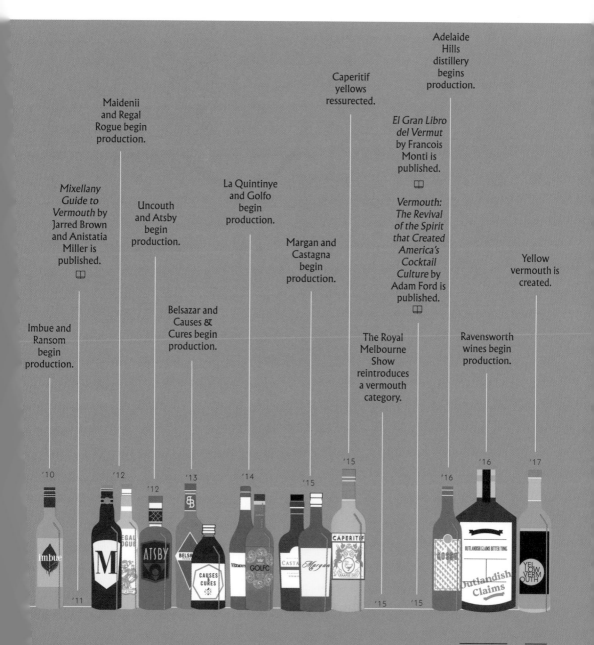

Imbue and Ransom begin production.

Mixellany Guide to Vermouth by Jarred Brown and Anistatia Miller is published.

Maidenii and Regal Rogue begin production.

Uncouth and Atsby begin production.

Belsazar and Causes & Cures begin production.

La Quintinye and Golfo begin production.

Margan and Castagna begin production.

Caperitif yellows ressurected.

The Royal Melbourne Show reintroduces a vermouth category.

El Gran Libro del Vermut by Francois Monti is published.

Vermouth: The Revival of the Spirit that Created America's Cocktail Culture by Adam Ford is published.

Adelaide Hills distillery begins production.

Ravensworth wines begin production.

Yellow vermouth is created.

'10 '12 '12 '13 '14 '15 '15 '15 '15 '16 '16 '17 '11

VERMOUTH AROUND THE WORLD

Aperitivo time – that lovely, languid half hour before dinner.

You decide to stroll to your favourite little wine bar in the corner of the city's main piazza and order a vermouth, chilled. Perhaps this evening you'll ask for it served with a dash of bitters to help stimulate the appetite even more. When you arrive, you discover you're not the only thirsty one; the bar is full of other patrons, all with glasses of vermouth in hand. This is a scene that takes place every day in countless bars across Italy. It has been taking place in Turin, virtually unchanged, for over 200 years.

Antonio Benedetto Carpano is credited with the creation of the first modern vermouth – a blend of wine, sugar and alcohol infused with herbs and spices – in a little wine shop opposite the Royal Palace in Turin's Piazza Castello in 1786.

He named his creation 'wermut' or 'vermuth', after the German word for wormwood, and it was a big hit with the burgeoning bourgeoisie in Turin. They came for the medicinal properties of this 'tonic wine', and stayed for the social enjoyment. Carpano's little shop soon thronged with eager customers, and had to start opening 24 hours a day to cater to the demand. It became the prototype for aperitivo bars across Italy and, soon, other producers jumped on the bandwagon: producers with now-famous names such as Cinzano and Martini. Turin became vermouth central, and these brands, even though production has mainly moved to other parts of Italy, still dominate the global market today.

Inspired by what was happening in Turin, the first French 'vermouths' were made in the first two decades of the nineteenth century by pioneering manufacturers Joseph Noilly in Lyons, and Joseph Chavasse in Chambery, just across the border from Turin in Savoie. The companies these two men founded – Noilly Prat and Dolin – are still major players in the market.

Unlike the traditional Italian style of vermouth, which is sweeter, darker and more bitter, the French style is drier, paler in appearance and relies more on its herbal characters.

As in Italy, vermouth is very much seen as an aperitif drink in France, but it has also become a fixture in France's culinary culture, lending its perfumed, anise-driven flavours to seafood dishes in particular, where it's used to deglaze pans, and in sauces.

The third major traditional vermouth-producing country is Spain, where the drink is known as 'vermut'. Production, mainly centred around Catalonia, started here in the late 1800s and, by the beginning of the twentieth century, vermut culture had reached its peak. The Café Torino, a spectacular Art Nouveau temple to the drink built in Barcelona in 1902, was designed by some of Barcelona's leading architects of the day, including Antoni Gaudi.

Spanish vermut tends to be richer and darker than its Italian or French counterparts, and has enjoyed a revival over the last few years. It is regularly served as an aperitif in tapas bars, over ice, with a slice of orange, an olive and a splash of soda water (club soda).

As the early Italian and French vermouth producers grew their businesses in the mid-nineteenth century, they started exporting, shipping to Sydney as early as the 1850s and New York in the 1860s. Americans took to vermouth enthusiastically, with bartenders latching on to its potential as a component in the newly fashionable mixed drinks called cocktails.

It's here, in America's bars, that vermouth cemented its place in global drinking culture as an essential component of now-classic cocktails such as the Martini (using the French dry style) and the Manhattan (using the sweeter Italian style), both created in the 1860s. Vermouth's popularity grew, surviving Prohibition and the Great Depression, powering cocktail culture until World War II.

The post-war generation, however, came to associate vermouth with their parents. Cocktails were seen as old-fogey drinks. Vermouth sales declined in the United States, and, although the category maintained steady sales in Europe – and enjoyed a burst of popularity in Australia in the 1970s – by the end of the millennium it looked as though vermouth's star was on the wane, with only a handful of large brands surviving.

Surprisingly, considering how far the drink had fallen out of fashion in that country, it was a handful of American craft producers that kick-started the revival of interest in high-quality vermouth in the early years of the twenty-first century, when makers such as Vya, Imbue and Atsby reasserted the primacy of vermouth as a standalone drink, not just a cocktail ingredient.

In the last few years other artisan producers, from South Africa to England, from Australia to Europe, have joined the revival, launching high-quality vermouths that take the classic Italian and French styles as a starting point and add twists and layers of regional individuality.

The large vermouth companies, now mostly owned by drinks multinationals (Noilly Prat and Martini & Rossi are both part of the huge Bacardi empire; Cinzano is a part of Gruppo Campari), have latched on to this revival by refreshing their brands, launching new products and increasing their marketing and promotional spend. As a result, the global market for vermouth is expected to grow to be worth US$19 billion by 2021.

There are a number of reasons for vermouth's comeback. The cocktail scene is thriving once more around the world, and the craft spirits industry – particularly the production of craft gin – is booming. Aperitivo time is back. And where cocktails are being mixed, where gin is being distilled and where aperitifs are being drunk, you'll find vermouth.

Drinkers – and booze producers – are becoming increasingly adventurous too; keen to explore strange new wines, and seek out new tastes and new flavour combinations. Essentially, to boldly go where no drinkers have gone before. And vermouth fits the adventurous bill splendidly: the drink is a blank canvas onto which the creative vermouth-maker can apply limitless permutations of wine, spirit, sweetness and botanicals.

– MAX ALLEN

VERMOUTH IN AUSTRALIA

Vermouth has a surprisingly long and rich history in Australia.

In the first half of the nineteenth century, before the development of a substantial local wine and spirit industry, vermouth was just one of many drinks imported by colonial merchants from Europe.

In 1855, *The Sydney Morning Herald* noted that Noilly vermouth was the 'favourite mark' in the market but, as it was in short supply, people were forced to drink brands of 'inferior quality'. Fine French vermouth was clearly popular among discerning drinkers.

Australian wineries started making their own vermouths in earnest during the second half of the nineteenth century, not only for domestic consumption, but also for potential export. In 1878, the Barossa Valley firm of Seppelt exhibited a vermouth from South Australia at the Exposition Universelle in Paris. These early vermouths, along with a startling array of other digestifs, including hops bitters and quinine champagne, were often marketed for their health-giving properties. Leading South Australian winery, Hardys, for example, advertised its vermouth in the 1880s as 'the purest tonic wine known'. We can guess what these old Australian vermouths tasted like because some of their recipes still exist. Current custodian of the family wine archives, Bill Seppelt, has his great-grandfather's handwritten blend books listing vermouth herbs and essences imported from Domenico Ulrich in Turin, Italy, WJ Bush & Co. in London, and detailing the other flavourings: oil of coriander, nutmeg, cardamom and thyme, which were added to sweet fortified base wines.

By the beginning of the twentieth century, all of Australia's larger, well-known wine firms – Seppelt, Hardys, Penfolds, Lindeman's and others – were making vermouth. Other, now-forgotten regional vineyards, such as Darveniza's Excelsior Vineyard in Victoria's Goulburn Valley, were also in the market, employing a winemaker from Bordeaux to produce vermouth and quinine wine. Independent wine merchants, such as Alexander and Paterson in Melbourne, also bottled their own vermouths at this time. Again, the marketing focus was often on the beneficial effects of consuming these drinks. Victorian Associated Vineyards' vermouth, consisting 'simply of wormwood, red flag, gentian, centaury and other herbs, skillfully combined with the juice of the Pedro Ximénez grape' was said to 'possess the properties of a bitter stomachic that acts like a charm, and frees the bowels from flatulency and pain'. Charming.

Another Victorian wine merchant to launch its own successful brand of vermouth around this time was the firm of Fabbri & Gardini of North Melbourne. Giuseppe Fabbri had fought with Garibaldi before coming to Australia in the 1870s. He and his business partner, Bruto Gardini, developed a range of wines and drinks including, in 1909, a brand of vermouth called Mont Buffalo – a full bottle of which is in the collection of the Italian Historical Society in Carlton. This is one of very few Australian-made vermouths not to shamelessly copy the French and Italian branding, but instead make reference to a local landmark, Mount Buffalo in Victoria's north-east, which became home to a large migrant Italian community.

Vermouth surged in popularity during the cocktail craze of the 1920s. As in the United States, it was an indispensable part of the Australian bartenders' arsenal, used in suddenly fashionable mixed drinks, such as the Martini – or Gin & French as it was often known in Australia – referring to the local preference for dry white, French-style vermouth rather than sweeter, Italian-style vermouth. In 1927, Barossa winery Yalumba responded to this new trend by releasing a pre-mixed cocktail of vermouth and gin called, creatively (if rather cheekily), Ver-Gin. And such was the demand for vermouth that in the 1930s major Italian brand Cinzano established a factory in Sydney to make its products for the Australian market.

Not surprisingly, sales of vermouth dipped during the years of the Depression and World War II, but, even though Australian wine drinkers had drifted away from the style by the 1950s, most of the big companies continued to produce it, albeit in reduced quantities. There were attempts to revive interest in the late 1960s, with Australian magazine *Australian Women's Weekly* recommending vermouth-based cocktails to serve at dinner parties, along with tantalising recipes for crumbed veal with vermouth and olives, pork chops with vermouth and prunes, and kidneys in vermouth sauce.

Something must have struck a chord because people developed a taste for vermouth once more in the 1970s, and vermouth producers began to compete more regularly in Australian wine shows. Renowned wine critic James Halliday remembers judging his first show in Sydney in 1974 and being given the vermouth class to assess, despite never having tasted vermouth before. Hardys' winemaker, Richard Warland, remembers judging the vermouths at a show around this time and finding a particular lemon flavour in the top-scoring entries, so he started adding some lemon essence to the Hardys vermouth and won gold the following year. John Angove, managing director of his family's winery in South Australia's Riverland region, remembers selling more of their Marko brand of vermouth in the 1970s than anything else at that time.

The booming Australian market led to the Italian firm Martini & Rossi engaging Yalumba to produce their vermouths under licence in the Barossa in the early 1970s. Yalumba's production manager, Peter Wall, remembers spending many happy months in Europe touring the Italian company's facilities – visits that often conveniently coincided with the ski season.

The most successful brand in the 1970s, however, was Cinzano, thanks in part to an extensive marketing campaign featuring legendary Australian tennis player, John Newcombe. In one print advertisement, the star even spruiked his 'own' cocktail, The Newk. He had come up with a grand-slam idea about Cinzano and invented a really original new highball in honour of himself. Why don't you join John in one? Put plenty of ice into a highball glass, then pour in one part Cinzano Rosso, one part Cinzano Bianco and two parts Cinzano Extra Dry. Top with dry ginger ale and stir gently. Garnish with a lemon wedge. Mention this to anyone who grew up glued to the TV during this era and they'll automatically recite the ad's catch phrase: 'Cin cin!'

Sales of vermouth began to decline throughout the 1980s and 90s as younger consumers became interested in other drinks: new, vermouth-less cocktails such as the Cosmopolitan, emerging cool-climate wines and craft beers.

Longstanding Australian vermouth brands disappeared from the shelves one by one; Angove's Marko managed to hang on until the late 2000s but, by the beginning of the current decade, De Bortoli, who sold their vermouth cheaply in 2 litre (68 fl oz) flagons, had what was left of the market for locally made products pretty much to themselves.

This is why, when premium Australian vermouths started appearing again in 2012, it seemed as though they had emerged from nowhere. To a whole generation of drinkers who had grown up with no experience of local vermouth, the category felt brand new. In fact, it's just the latest, exciting chapter in a very old story.

– MAX ALLEN

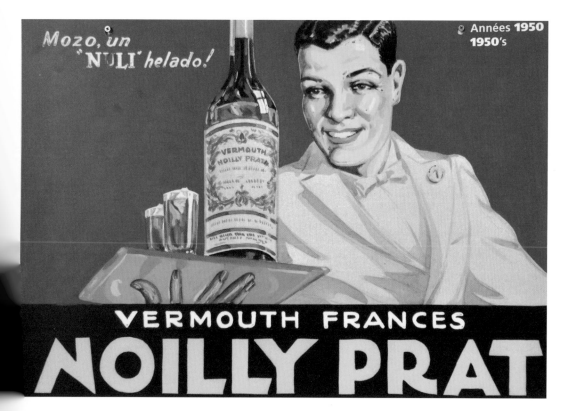

GRAPES

Many different grape varieties can form the base wine for vermouth.

When making a large volume of vermouth, producers will source grapes from large-producing regions, whereas more artisanal vermouths will often use local grapes varieties. Traditionally, vermouth was made with white grapes but, increasingly in contemporary vermouth production, red grapes are used.

Muscat was a very popular grape used in the Industrial Age, particularly in Piedmont, Italy. The Muscat family is quite large, with the most aromatic variety being the Muscat à Petits Grains or Frontignan Muscat. Muscat Ottonel, Moscato Giallo, Muscat of Alexandria (or Zibibbo) and other varietals are all good candidates for vermouth base wines. Muscats are grown everywhere in the wine world, producing some well-known sweet wines like Vin de Constance in South Africa, the famous Muscat in Rutherglen, north-east Victoria, and Zibibbo di Pantelleria in Italy.

In the late nineteenth and early twentieth centuries, as producers increased the volume of their production, there was not enough local Muscat and other native grape varieties to meet the demand. Martini, for example, turned to **Trebbiano** and **Catarratto** for the bulk of their production, using high-yield grapes from areas like Emilia-Romagna, Puglia and Sicily, which made the final product more affordable. In their more recent Riserva, Martini use the local **Langhe Nebbiolo** or **Moscato d'Asti.**

Moscato from Asti, a region of Italy famous for its sparkling wine, was the original grape used by Carpano, and it is still used today along with a larger proportion of grapes from Sicily due to the high demand for Moscato. Cocchi, based in Asti, still uses Moscato.

On the other side of the Alps, Dolin was using the local **Jacquère**, which gives a crisp wine and, today, is commonly blended with **Ugni Blanc**. Ugni Blanc, known internationally as Trebbiano, is a neutral, high-yield grape used primarily in south-west France to produce Cognac. In Italy, it is the second-most planted white grape variety. Its synonyms, or other known names, are **Thalia** in Portugal, **St-Emilion** in California or Trebbiano with different clones. In the south of France, Noilly Pratt consistently uses **Clairette** and **Piquepoul**: two white grapes grown locally around Montpellier. These varieties are considered 'secondary grapes' as they are not among the original 'noble' varieties. Clairette is famous in the Drôme near Montélimar for the ancestral sparkling Clairette de Die, and Piquepoul, in particular, is the base for an Appellation d'Origine Contrôlée (AOC) wine called Piquepoul de Pinet, which is undergoing something of a revival at the moment.

In Bordeaux, Lillet uses **Sauvignon** and **Semillon**; varieties that are well known to wine drinkers. These two form the base of the best Sauternes wines and most dry Bordeaux whites. Sauvignon, in particular, is very popular nowadays, either with Sancerre or in Marlborough, New Zealand, where it is used in a completely different style. Semillon grown in the Hunter Valley near Sydney also has its followers.

In Spain, vermouths are often produced from the white grape **Macabeu**, or its synonym in **Rioja**, Viura. Macabeu is by far the main white variety in Rioja, but it is also very popular in the north of Spain and on the other side of the Pyrenees, in France. It is rare to see the noble **Albarino** from Galicia used in vermouth, but St. Petroni use it in theirs. Vermouths from sherry producers are derived from the local grape **Palomino** or **Pedro Ximénez** once they have been made into sherry. Oloroso sherry is the most commonly used base wine in Andalusian *vermut*, such as Lustau or Gonzalez Byass. In Spain, red grapes are also becoming popular, with **Tempranillo** and **Garnacha** commonly being used in vermouth production. Tempranillo is at its best in the Rioja region, and can be found as Tinta Roriz in Portugal, while Garnacha is found everywhere in Spain and also in the south of France where it is called Grenache, and in Sardinia, where it is called Cannonau. Tempranillo produces some basic wines as well as some exceptional wines like Vega Sicilia from Ribera del Duero and Grenache at Chateau Rayas in Châteauneuf-du-Pape.

Newer producers are a lot more experimental with grapes. In Germany, Belsazar represents the new generation of vermouth on The Old Continent.

The word vermouth comes from the German *wermut*, and *Wermutwein* was a common medieval drink. Belsazar vermouth uses local grapes such as Spätburgunder (**Pinot Noir**), **Gewürztraminer** and **Chasselas**, depending on the style of vermouth. Currently, Pinot Noir as a wine grape is the height of fashion worldwide, and the benchmark is unquestionably Burgundy reds such as Musigny or Romanée-Conti. Gewürztraminer, with its Germanic spelling, is grown mostly in Alsace, in France, followed by Germany and Italy, but the variety – also called Traminer – is present in many countries, from Australia to the United States and even Japan and Israel. Chasselas is mostly known as a table grape as it was in fashion among the kings of France around the sixteenth to seventeenth centuries. It is the most planted white grape variety in Switzerland and is largely used in wine production around Lake Geneva (*Lac Léman*) between Geneva and Lausanne, the Valais, and the Neuchâtel region.

In the United States, some producers such as Vya on the West Coast have based their blend on traditional European varieties, such as Tempranillo and Muscat. One producer, Ransom, based in Oregon, uses **Riesling**, **Chardonnay** and Pinot Noir.

Riesling is popular among new producers of vermouth. It is considered a 'noble' variety, which in winemaking terms means it is revered for its high quality and its expression of the site on which it is planted. The best expression of Riesling is found on the Rhine river in Alsace and in Germany's Mosel Valley. This important grape variety can produce both the driest and sweetest styles of wine, such as Eiswein in Germany.

Riesling is very important in Central Europe for its vast acreage, and is now found everywhere in the world. South Australia also has a certain reputation for their Riesling, which was introduced by German colonial settlers in the nineteenth century in the Barossa and Clare valleys. Duncan Forsyth, at Mount Edward in the Otago region of New Zealand, has made a vermouth based on Riesling, following in the Rhine tradition of wormwood wine.

Many wine producers in Oregon (United States) are welcoming the Burgundian variety of Pinot Noir, and are also embracing Chardonnay with enthusiasm. Chardonnay is probably the most well-known wine grape on the planet now. Originally from Burgundy, this white variety has been planted with success in many parts of the world as it adapts very well to different conditions. Despite this, Burgundy still remains the benchmark for Chardonnay with its great wines from Chablis and Côte de Beaune, including the Montrachet. On the East Coast of the United States, you'll find Uncouth using local wines from Long Island or Finger Lakes. Atsby, the first vermouth produced in New York, uses Chardonnay from Long Island. The Caperitif, from Swartland in South Africa, is based on an old quinquina recipe and is now using a blend of **Chenin Blanc** and **Frontignan Muscat**. These two varieties have been planted successfully for some time in South Africa. Some old Chenin Blanc vines in particular are producing some very fine wines under the synonym of Steen.

Chenin Blanc has its origin in the Loire Valley where it is used to produce a vast array of wine styles, from sparkling to dry white and sweet Botrytis wines. The famous names of Vouvray, Bonnezeaux and Quarts de Chaume in Anjou are inseparable from their wines, produced from Chenin Blanc grapes. Chenin is a difficult grape to grow because of its sensitivity to disease in more humid climates, but New Zealand producers such as Milton have produced some excellent wines using this grape, and its popularity is growing in Australia too.

Possibly the most experimental approach is seen in Australia, where **Viognier**, **Syrah** and **Cabernet Sauvignon** are used to produce Maidenii; **Sangiovese** and Viognier for Causes & Cures; Chenin Blanc and **Grenache** for Adelaide Hills; **Roussanne** and Viognier for Castagna; Hunter Semillon, Barossa Semillon and **Shiraz** for Regal Rogue and Grenache and **Pinot Gris** for Ravensworth.

Viognier is a white aromatic variety from the Northern Rhône valley where it almost became extinct in the 1970s. Château-Grillet is one of the most famous wines from this area, and has grown in popularity since the beginning of the twenty-first century, witnessing a revival in the south of France as well as in California, New Zealand and Australia. It is also mixed with Syrah in small proportions to produce fine red wines such as those in Côte-Rôtie.

Syrah, also known as Shiraz, **Serine** and, in the past, **Hermitage**, is another red variety from the Rhône valley. The wines from the Hill of Hermitage have given notoriety to this variety but, more recently, countries such as Australia have experimented with it to great success, producing such wines as Hill of Grace from Henschke. Syrah is rarely used in vermouth production as the colour can be very dark, but it is well suited to the production of rosé.

SANGIOVESE
& VIOGNIER

VIOGNIER,
SYRAH &
CABERNET
SAUVIGNON

CHENIN
BLANC &
GRENACHE

HUNTER
SEMILLON,
BAROSSA
SEMILLON &
SHIRAZ

ROUSSANNE
& VIOGNIER

Cabernet Sauvignon is probably the least likely candidate for vermouth production as it is a tannic red variety. The best example of Cabernet use is from the Medoc in Bordeaux, but California has also developed a strong reputation for producing fine wines using Cabernet Sauvignon. This variety is very popular in vineyards all over the world, and has been produced in Chile since the nineteenth century. More recently, it has been produced in the Bolgheri region of Italy, in Australia, the North Island of New Zealand and even China. Sangiovese is another unlikely candidate for vermouth as it is quite a savoury and tannic grape. This Tuscan variety is also grown in many wine regions of Italy where different clones are planted, and it is present in Corsica and Argentina too. Recently, Sangiovese was exported and grown in parts of California and Australia.

Roussanne, a white variety from the Rhône valley, has a limited production in Australia, but documents show its presence in the late nineteenth century at Yeringberg in the Yarra Valley. Alongside **Marsanne**, it is famous for its use in white Hermitage wines.

Pinot Gris belongs to the large Pinot family and is most famous in Alsace for dry, textural white varieties, as well as late-harvest Botrytis wines. More recently, Italy has put **Pinot Grigio** on the map for its fresher white wine style.

This non-exhaustive list shows that the possibilities are endless for vermouth production, and that the grape variety used is dictated primarily by local supply and what will best suit the style of the final wine. It is important to highlight how different this traditional approach is to that of industrial vermouth production, where volume and cost are prioritised and, consequently, the grapes used are from high-yield areas on productive land. In contrast, we can broadly say that the new generation of vermouth producers around the world are sourcing grapes from high-quality wine regions, as exemplified by Belsazar in the Baden region, Ransom in Oregon, Atsby in Long Island and Maidenii in Heathcote.

With grapes comes the notion of AOC, or Geographical Indication (GI). But, so far, the only vermouth with a GI is Vermouth di Torino, with the only stipulation being that Italian wine must be used. DOC, or DOCG from Piedmont, can be declared if the vermouth is made with more than 20 per cent volume of Italian wine. Vermouth de Chambery was a protected AOC, but with only one major producer and one marginal producer now in operation, this GI is no longer recognised in Europe. Vermouth regulation deals more with vermouth production, but, in my view, the choice of grapes used is equally important.

THE RULES

Vermouth is a highly-regulated wine, particularly in Europe.

According to the International Organisation of Vine and Wine (OIV), wine is defined as 'the beverage resulting exclusively from the partial or complete alcoholic fermentation of fresh grapes, whether crushed or not, or of grape must. Its actual alcohol content shall not be less than 8.5 per cent volume. Nevertheless, taking into account climate, soil, vine variety, special qualitative factors or traditions specific to certain vineyards, the minimum total alcohol content may be able to be reduced to 7 per cent volume by legislation particular to the region considered'.

Vermouth also belongs to a subcategory of wine known as 'fortified wine'. These wines are made by adding spirit at particular stages of production depending on the style and desired effect. Also in this category are drinks such as Port, sherry, Madeira, apera, topaque and the less popular Vin Doux Naturel (VDN), including Rivesaltes, Maury and Banyuls, and Vin de Liqueur (VDL), including Pineau des Charentes and Floc de Gascogne. However, being 'aromatised', vermouth goes one step further with the addition of botanicals from various parts of plants, including leaves, fruits, roots, flowers and stems. The resulting wine is bittersweet.

AROMATISED WINE

Aromatised wine is defined by the OIV as:

1 / obtained from at least 75 per cent by volume of wine and/or special wine, as defined in the OIV's International Code of Oenological Practices, and which has undergone an aromatisation process;

2 / to which ethyl alcohol of viticultural origin and/or a wine distillate and/or alcohol of agricultural origin could have been added;

3 / which could have undergone a sweetening;

4 / which could have undergone a colouring;

5 / which could have undergone one or more of other specific oenological practices applicable to this beverage;

6 / with an actual alcoholic strength by volume varying between 14.5 per cent minimum and 22 per cent maximum.

VERMOUTH IN THE EU

Within 'Aromatised wines' is another subcategory for 'Vermouth'. It states that the specificity of the final product must meet the following technical parameters outlined by the European Union (EU) regulation (Regulation No. 251/2014):

1 / alcohol volume between 14.5 per cent minimum and 22 per cent maximum;

2 / a minimum of 75 per cent wine;

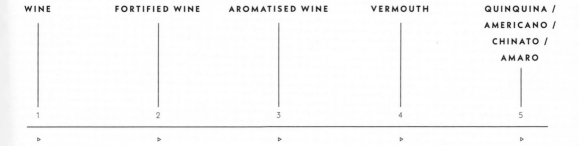

WINE	FORTIFIED WINE	AROMATISED WINE	VERMOUTH	QUINQUINA / AMERICANO / CHINATO / AMARO
1	2	3	4	5

3 / includes spirit;

4 / characteristic taste has been obtained by the use of appropriate substances of *Artemisia* species;

5 / watering, colouring, sweetening and other aromatisation are allowed but not mandatory.

VERMOUTH IN THE US

United States legislation for vermouth production differs a little bit from the rest of the world.

According to the US Alcohol and Tobacco Tax and Trade Bureau (TTB) section 21, class 7, of Regulations No. 4, 'Aperitif' wine is defined as 'wine having an alcoholic content of not less than 15 per cent by volume, compounded from grape wine containing added brandy or alcohol, flavoured with herbs and other natural aromatic flavouring materials'. Vermouth is further defined as 'a type of aperitif wine, compounded from grape wine, having the taste, aroma and characteristics generally attributed to vermouth'. The use of *Artemisia* species, in particular wormwood, is limited in order to create a final product that is free of thujone, a compound that is said to cause hallucinations. It is important to note that wormwood is not the only botanical that contains thujone; it is also found in plants such as sage, mugwort, juniper and oregano. Because of this regulation, many American vermouth producers do not use *Artemisia*, with some exceptions, including Uncouth, who use mugwort (*A. vulgaris*) instead of wormwood (*A. absinthium*).

NOT QUITE VERMOUTH

Some aromatised wines are not classified as vermouth because of the specific wines or botanicals used to produce them. These include:

QUINQUINA WINE
whose main flavour is natural quinine.

AMERICANO
whose flavour is created by natural flavouring substances derived from wormwood and gentian, and whose colour has been achieved using authorised yellow and/or red colourings.

BAROLO CHINATO
made using wine from the Barolo GI, and whose main flavour is natural quinine.

BITTER VINO
whose main flavour is natural gentian, and whose colour has been achieved using authorised yellow and/or red colourings.

AMARO
some of which are made using a vermouth base unlike most amari, which are based on spirit.

The root of the word 'vermouth' is German, but it is now known by many names.

Other terms are often associated with vermouth and found on vermouth labels, but are not regulated. These include:

ROSSO, ROJO AND ROUGE
which indicate a sweet vermouth in what is referred to as the Torino style.

ROSATO, ROSADO AND ROSÉ
which are relatively new terms used to describe a lighter style of vermouth.

BIANCO, BLANCO AND BLANC
refer to a sweet vermouth with no addition of caramel.

RISERVA, GRAN RISERVA, CLASSIC, CLÁSSICO, OLD VINE, AMBRATO AND AMBRE
are other names often present on labels, and refer to a particular style for each brand.

No matter where it is produced, vermouth always starts with wine, and wine starts with grapes (see page 26). Some might say that wine is just a drink. Well, it is once it's in the glass but, before that, a lot of choices have had to be made. The first decision is about picking the grapes. In the Palaeolithic era, our ancestors had to scale trees to reach the climbing wild vines. Now, with viticulture, or the cultivation of grapes, we are able to pick the grapes using machinery. This technology has been developed over the past 30 years and is always improving. Some grapes are still picked manually, often in smaller plantings and on difficult sites at high-end vineyards. Once the grapes have been picked, they can be pressed, crushed and de-stemmed or simply unloaded into a fermenting vessel.

Fermentation technology is rapidly evolving, but many producers have come back to ancestral methods. From the modern supremacy of stainless steel and hospital-grade hygiene, we are now seeing a return to wood and terracotta, with more traditional practice and less input. While the progression of biotechnology has generated better understanding of the fermentation processes amongst producers, it has also led to the creation of more additives. With many production options available, the winemaker must have a clear idea of the final product in order to select the best method to achieve the desired wine.

The most critical stage in vermouth production is the extraction of botanicals for their aromatics and bitterness. You can extract the botanicals using wine, spirit or both. Aromatics can also be extracted using distillation. Each extraction method will yield different results, as will the seasonality and regionality of the botanicals. For example, I noticed this year's aniseed myrtle was a lot more powerful than in 2016 despite using the same extraction method. Similarly, Seville oranges from Mornington, in Victoria, are more bitter than those from Mildura.

The particularity of vermouth is its use of the plant that gave the drink its name: wormwood. European Union legislation actually specifies it must not only be wormwood, but a plant from the *Artemisia* genus. As you will discover in the following chapter, Wormwood (see page 38), the *Artemisia* family is quite large.

wermut

GERMANY

vermouth

AUSTRALIA, UK & US

vermout

CHAMBERY

vermú

SPAIN

vermut

SPAIN & ITALY

wermoed

THE NETHERLANDS

PRODUCTION

It is impossible to generalise the way vermouth is made, so we will illustrate the production with two different examples.

DOLIN

Dolin has been making vermouth in France since the early nineteenth century. The company is owned by the Sevez family who acquired Dolin in 1919, and to this day they prepare their dry vermouth using the original recipe from 1821. In the early days of its production, Dolin used local wine in their vermouth, but now the majority comes from further afield and is bought as bulk-finished wine, which is finished wine that has not yet been bottled and can be bought en masse in a tanker. Dolin argues that the base wine needs to be as neutral as possible – a sentiment shared by many large producers.

1 — The botanicals are combined with the white wine in a tanker and left to macerate. The mixture is stirred daily before the aromatic wine is filtered out and the botanicals discarded.

2 — Sugar is dissolved in water, then the sugar mixture and alcohol are added to the aromatic white wine.

3 — Fining and discolouring follows, then refrigeration to allow the precipitation of the potassium bitartrate crystals.

4 — The vermouth is then refrigerated and filtered to remove any remaining solids.

5 — A small amount of sulphur dioxide is finally added to preserve the freshness of the vermouth.

6 — The vermouth is tested in the laboratory to ensure both correct composition and alcohol content of 17.5 per cent alcohol by volume.

7 — Just before bottling, a small dose of metatartaric acid is added to avoid precipitation of potassium bitartrate crystals.

8 — The vermouth is then bottled, sealed and labelled to create Dolin dry vermouth.

MAIDENII

At Maidenii in Australia we use a more contemporary method to produce our vermouth. The fact that vermouth is made up of at least 75 per cent wine led us to consider the wine as an important factor in the production. We decided to source the grapes from a high-quality region and control the production of the base wine. In winemaking, simplicity is key and minimal intervention is best practice. We also considered the selection of grapes in relation to the different styles of vermouth. Let's take Maidenii Classic as an example. This vermouth is a medium-dry style with a rose colour made using Syrah grapes from the Heathcote GI, which are well regarded for red wine production.

1 ———— The grapes are picked by hand to limit colour extraction before being transported to the press for whole-bunch pressing, with no crushing, again to limit colour extraction. Slow pressing allows us to extract the pink juice in its best condition. At this stage, the temperature is controlled between 15–20°C (59–68°F) to ferment with natural yeast.

2 ———— The next step is crucial: the fortification during fermentation. To do this, we add the spirit at the precise moment to obtain the final level of sugar in the vermouth. This operation needs to be monitored very closely by continual analysis of the fermentation.

3 ———— Another key part of this process is the introduction of botanicals via a spirit. Botanicals macerate individually in spirit for 1–2 months. They are then blended to create the spirit 'mother-tincture', which varies depending on the style. Once this mother-tincture has been added and the vermouth has been fortified, it has all its ingredients. No sugar is added for sweetness, and no caramel for colouring. At this stage, the vermouth is left to mature and clarify for a few months.

4 ———— The vermouth is then filtered prior to bottling with only a minimal addition of sulphur dioxide.

5 ———— The wine is then bottled, labelled and ready for consumption.

We are bottling a small amount of the same wine, but unfiltered. Producing vermouth in this way offers a more natural approach, without the need for filtration and with very little sulphur. This method more closely reflects the way vermouth was originally made, and the difference in intensity of the finished product is very interesting.

SPIRIT

Archaeological discoveries have revealed that vermouth's early 'ancestor' was not made with spirit as it was not available.

Some traditional producers, such as Dolin, still prefer to macerate their botanicals in wine. The development of distillation by Arab alchemists in the ninth century, though mostly used for medicinal and aromatic purposes, brought a new dimension to the world of vermouth. Spirit helps to stabilise vermouth by increasing its alcohol content to a level where sugar can no longer easily ferment, and it also decreases the effects of oxidation.

Like the production of perfume, the main feature of vermouth is its botanicals, and the art is in the extraction of these essences and the ways in which they are combined. Spirit has a greater power of extraction as compared to wine due to its much higher level of alcohol. It can be added to wine during fermentation to create a *mistelle* (a partially fermented grape juice retaining a lot of natural sweetness), which can be used as a blending component in the production of vermouth and other products. Spirit can also be added to finished wine before the addition of the botanicals. Most new and industrial brands will extract botanicals' properties in neutral spirit at 96 per cent or spirit diluted to around 50 per cent. However some producers, such as Noilly Prat, macerate their botanicals in a blend of wine and spirit, leaving it to mature in wooden *foudres*, or large wooden vats.

According to EU authority (Regulation No. 251/2014), the only alcohols authorised as an addition to aromatised wines are:

(a) ethyl alcohol of agricultural origin, as defined in Annex I, point 1, to Regulation (EC) No. 110/2008, including viticultural origin;

(b) wine alcohol or dried grape alcohol;

(c) wine distillate or dried grape distillate;

(d) distillate of agricultural origin, as defined in Annex I, point 2, to Regulation (EC) No. 110/2008;

(e) wine spirit, as defined in Annex II, point 4, to Regulation (EC) No. 110/2008;

(f) grape-marc spirit, as defined in Annex II, point 6, to Regulation (EC) No. 110/2008;

(g) spirit drinks distilled from fermented dried grapes.

'Agricultural origin' can refer to grain, corn, grapes, sugar beets, sugarcane, tubers or other fermented plant material.

Another way of extracting aromatics from botanicals is distillation, but this method is rarely used. Martini & Rossi combine all these methods and, being part of a big spirit group, have access to a cheap supply of gin in which to macerate the plants. Popular spirits such as whisky, absinthe, vodka, cognac and rum all have the potential to be used in vermouth.

SUGAR

Sweetness is an important dimension in vermouth, primarily to balance bitterness, which is often perceived as unpleasant.

Sweetness can be derived from several ingredients, but the main one is the fruit itself. Grapes contain a large amount of sugar in the form of glucose and fructose that, when fermented, converts to alcohol. With the addition of a spirit (fortification technique), fermentation is halted and natural sugar is retained. Few vermouth producers use this technique as it makes it difficult to reach precise alcohol and sugar levels, and it also dictates the timing of vermouth-making, confining it to vintage time. Maidenii is one of the few vermouth producers that uses this technique. The alternative is to add sugar, as it is allowed for any vermouth made using this technique. Should you wish to add sugar, the questions remain: which sugar, when to add it, and how much?

The list of sweetening agents is long, but the EU authority (Regulation No. 251/2014) has limited vermouth to the following:

(a) semi-white sugar, white sugar, extra-white sugar, dextrose, fructose, glucose syrup, sugar solution, invert sugar solution, invert sugar syrup, as defined in Council Directive 2001/111/EC (1);

(b) grape must, concentrated grape must and rectified concentrated grape must, as defined in points 10, 13 and 14 of Part II of Annex VII to Regulation (EU) No. 1308/2013;

(c) burned sugar, which is a product obtained exclusively from the controlled heating of sucrose without bases, mineral acids or other chemical additives;

(d) honey as defined in Council Directive 2001/110/EC (2);

(e) carob syrup;

(f) any other natural carbohydrate substances having a similar effect to those products.

Depending on the producer's method, sugar can be added to wine, water, spirit, or all of these together. It is interesting to note as well that most vermouths are coloured by caramel, and this caramel also plays a role not only in the appearance of the finished vermouth, but its sweetness and even aromatics. The quantity of sugar used is a matter of taste and, importantly, style.

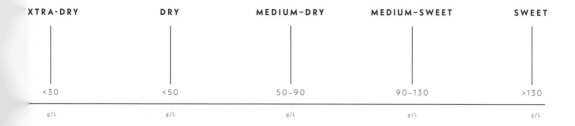

XTRA-DRY	DRY	MEDIUM-DRY	MEDIUM-SWEET	SWEET
<30	<50	50-90	90-130	>130
g/L	g/L	g/L	g/L	g/L

WORMWOOD

I first learned about wormwood as an ingredient in absinthe, the spirit that, when consumed, made reality slip away and the 'green fairy' take hold.

This, of course, makes a young bartender want to try the stuff, or at least find out more about it. A little bit of research revealed that absinthe was in fact banned for a number of years in a number of countries, including France and the United States.

A little more research, and you can read some outlandish stories on why it was banned, including the story of Jean Lanfray who, after drinking two glasses of absinthe, shot his wife and children. The story also goes that in addition to the two glasses of absinthe, Lanfray also consumed the following preceding the tragedy:

1 crème de menthe and 1 brandy with breakfast,
6 glasses of wine with lunch,
1 glass of wine for a knock-off beverage,
1 coffee (with brandy, of course) for a pre-dinner aperitif,
1 litre of wine with dinner,
and 1 coffee after dinner (this time with marc in it).

So maybe it wasn't all down to the absinthe after all.

Still, this was the story that ushered in the ban of absinthe for quite some time and, up until the last decade or so, the United States still had a ban on absinthe. In fact, absinthe doesn't make you hallucinate (sorry!). It does however usually hover around 70 per cent ABV, which is the reason for people's reckless behaviour while drinking the stuff. Because of its high proof, absinthe produces GABA inhibitors, which slow the firing of the synapses, meaning the brain can fire more freely.

Artemisia absinthium, or Grand Wormwood, is used in vermouth, as well as in absinthe. In fact, it is required that vermouth use at least a species of the *Artemisia* genus in order to be called a vermouth under EU legislation. Further to that, the GI of Vermouth de Torino (vermouth from the Torino region of Italy) states that the *A. absinthium* or *A. pontica* (another species of *Artemisia*) used should be from the Piedmont region of Italy. The United States has a different take on what constitutes vermouth, though, saying that, there is no mention of wormwood in their legislation around vermouth, which is why some American brands produce vermouth minus the wormwood. In Australia, there are even fewer regulations, although most if not all Australian vermouth contains wormwood. As the industry grows, I would hazard a guess that rules similar to those outlined in EU legislation will be introduced here.

Besides being mandatory under the law, there are other reasons why vermouth producers use wormwood in their vermouths. One, is the level of bitterness. For young bartenders the importance of balancing sweet, sour and bitter flavours in cocktails cannot be overstated, and it's one of the first things they learn how to do.

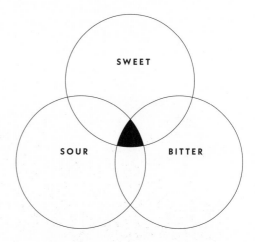

The base of vermouth is wine, which has acid, and sugar, which has sugar! A third element needs to be added to ensure harmony of flavour, and that is wormwood. This botanical is perfect because, unlike a lot of other bitter plants, it has an amazing aromatic profile. Think soft anise, mint and sage all rolled into one, lifted with the smell of fresh orange flowers. Wormwood not only balances out everything else in vermouth, it also provides the backbone for those flavours to sit on. Wormwood in vermouth is like music at a party; without it a party doesn't have the same ambience, but with it everything seems to flow.

The best way to source wormwood is to forage for it, but be sure to take someone with you who can easily identify the plant.

The genus of *Artemisia* contains around 350 different species, some of which have been used medicinally for a long time. Going back as early as 1500 BC, *Artemisia* was used with wine to treat digestive problems. Fast forward to today and people still plant *A. absinthium* near chook pens so chickens can eat the wormwood when they get worms. In 2015, Chinese scientist Tu Youyou shared the Nobel Prize in Physiology or Medicine for her research into artemisinin, a key ingredient in antimalarial drugs. In native North American medicine, Gray Sagewort (*A. ludoviciana*) is used to treat sore throats, Capillary Wormwood (*A. abrotanum*) to treat menstrual cramps and Tarragon (*A. dracunculus*) to treat jaundice. The list goes on and on, but my favourite use of *Artemisia* is *A. dracunculus* for the treatment of hunger.

BÉARNAISE SAUCE

A. dracunculus, or tarragon as it is more widely known, is the main ingredient in béarnaise sauce, which I like to pour liberally over grilled porterhouse steak. This is how I prepare said medicine.

SERVES 2

100 ml (3½ fl oz) **extra-dry vermouth** (I use Maidenii dry vermouth)

30 ml (1 fl oz) **apple-cider vinegar**

5 g (⅛ oz) **dried pepperberries, crushed**

2 **egg yolks**

100 g (3½ oz) **salted butter, cubed**

pinch of chopped tarragon leaves

Combine the vermouth, vinegar and pepperberries in a small saucepan and bring to the boil over medium–high heat. Reduce the heat to medium and simmer for 5 minutes, then strain through a fine-mesh sieve and set aside to cool completely.

Add the egg yolks to the vermouth mixture and whisk to combine. Transfer the mixture to a double-boiler and set over medium–low heat. Add the butter, 10 g (¼ oz) at a time, whisking constantly until combined. Add the tarragon and whisk for another minute. Remove from the heat and serve immediately over grilled porterhouse steak.

WORMWOOD THROUGH THE EYES OF A BOTANIST

Artemisia is what most people would call a 'daisy bush'. The crushed grey-green leaves are aromatic, and not always pleasantly so, hinting at the rich pharmacopoeia inside that so excites Shaun and Gilles. *A. absinthium* – the most popular choice for a bitter additive to liquor – grows naturally in poor soils in northern Africa, Europe and surrounding areas, but has become established as a weed elsewhere in the world. The other 350 or so species are found mostly in Northern Hemisphere countries, but also South Africa and South America and, these days, in our parks and gardens. Apart from their contributions to the vermouth and absinthe industries, wormwoods provide a handy and hardy plant for drought-stressed gardens in southern Australia. So tough, they sometimes stray beyond the walls: *A. arborescens*, or Silver Wormwood, has become established in New South Wales and South Australia, while *A. verlotiorum*, or Chinese Wormwood, is an occasional invasive on roadsides around Melbourne.

Named after Artemisia II, botanist and Queen of Caria (part of modern-day Turkey) in the fourth century BC, *Artemisia* has been ascribed many uses. The queen apparently attributed menstruation-promoting properties to a species of *Artemisia*, a link to her namesake, the Greek god Artemis, who reigned over the moon and therefore regulated earthly cycles. Such properties may have been caused by what we now call sesquiterpenoids, the active ingredient in the most widely used antimalarial drug in use today. A clue to the possible function of this molecule was written up during the latter part of the Chinese Han Dynasty, around 200 BC, and suggested this species was useful in the treatment of intermittent fevers, which are typical of malaria.

– TIM ENTWISLE

WORMWOOD GIN

Sebastian Raeburn also loves wormwood, perhaps almost as much as I do. He makes a gin called Anther; a delightful drop that uses wormwood in its botanical makeup. In fact, many of the botanicals you find in gin also appear in vermouth. Gin is the vermouth of the spirit world and vermouth is the gin of the wine world. If you can't get your hands on a bottle of Anther, fear not; this recipe yields a wonderfully wormwoody result.

MAKES 700 ML (23½ FL OZ)

1 × 700 ml (23½ fl oz) **bottle of London dry gin** (Beefeater is a good start)

20 g (¾ oz) **freshly chopped wormwood**

Combine the gin and wormwood in a large airtight container, cover and leave to macerate for 45 minutes at room temperature.

Strain the gin through a fine-mesh sieve into a sterilised glass bottle or jar (see page 78) and discard the wormwood.

Mix and drink vigorously.

TRADITIONAL BOTANICALS

Before I knew about vermouth, I knew about gin. I was behind the bar at Gin Palace in Melbourne, drinking in as much information as I could, so to speak.

One thing that brings gin and vermouth together (besides the Martini, of course) is the use of botanicals to flavour and aromatise. Initially, the botanicals in both products were used for medicinal purposes. In 1269, Jacob van Maerlant wrote in *Der Naturen Bloeme* that a recipe combining boiled rainwater or wine with juniper berries could be used to treat stomach pain. Many believe (as do I) that this is the origin of gin. Later, botanicals were used to cover up the unpleasant taste of alcohol as both drinks began to be consumed for their alcohol content rather than their beneficial ingredients. In the case of vermouth, its life really began during the Industrial Age, when ingenuity reigned and people added herbs, sugar and alcohol to wine that

had gone off to make it more palatable and increase its shelf life. Ingredients were sourced from the immediate environment, creating the unique and characteristic flavours, or *terroir*, of the earliest vermouths.

While this doesn't give a glorified history of vermouth, it does show how local ingredients informed its flavour. Nowadays, vermouth-makers source botanicals from all over the world. We do this at Maidenii too, but the heart of the product, in my opinion at least, should always evoke a sense of place. A clear example of this is in the traditional vermouths of Turin and the surrounding north of Italy, whose botanical blends are made of ingredients that are commonly available in the area, including wormwood and juniper. The historic availability of more exotic spices through the nearby port of Genoa also gave early producers access to rarities such as vanilla, which is a key flavour in the Italian Carpano Antica Formula.

When we first created Maidenii vermouth we generated a list of over 200 native and traditional plants that we wanted to use. From there, we categorised them into the different parts of a plant, as these offer similar qualities. This really helped us to understand the influence of not only the flavours of individual plants but their different components too. We were left with a list of roots, barks, flowers, fruits, leaves and seeds and, from there, selected our super-secret 34 botanicals, and the core range of Maidenii vermouths was born.

*roots, barks,
flowers,
fruits, leaves
and seeds*

roots

The primary reason we use roots in vermouth is to add bitterness at extremely high levels.

The root of *Gentiana lutea*, for example, is so bitter that it can be still detected when diluted by 12,000 parts to 1. This extreme sensitivity may be due to the human aversion to bitter flavours. Through years of evolution, our tastebuds have come to recognise bitterness as a potential toxin and are programmed to alert us to its presence. This might explain why it took a few tries before you learned to love the taste of beer or Campari. The upside of this fact is that when we do have something bitter, the brain identifies it as a poison and speeds up the metabolism to help the body digest it. This is why our favourite after-dinner drinks or aperitifs usually contain something bitter. To create a palatable vermouth, you are looking for a balance between the sweet and sour base ingredients and the bitterness of roots to round out the holy trinity.

COMMON GENTIAN PREPARATION

This very old recipe for a simple liquid preparation to treat stomach ailments was taken from the *Experimental History of the Materia Medica* by William Lewis (1791).

MAKES 425 ML (14½ FL OZ)

28 g (1 oz) **gentian root**
28 g (1 oz) **fresh lemon zest**
16 g (½ oz) **dried orange zest**

Add 425 ml (14½ fl oz) water to a saucepan and bring to the boil over medium–high heat. Add the gentian root and lemon and orange zest, then reduce the heat to medium–low and simmer for 1 hour to infuse.

Strain through a fine-mesh sieve into a sterilised glass jar or bottle (see page 78) and store in the refrigerator for up to 2 weeks.

GENTIAN (GENTIANA LUTEA, G. SCABRA)

Bitter, bitter, bitter, but lovely. Gentian is an alpine flower native to central and southern Europe, whose extremely bitter root is harvested and dried for use in a whole spectrum of alcohols. It is used in the production of divine gentian liqueurs such as Suze and Salers as well as Americanos, a subsection of aromatised wines. Likewise, most cocktail bitters you pick up will contain gentian root. Being the benchmark bittering agent, gentian has also been used for a long time to treat stomach problems. To this day, I find having a small serve (10 ml/¼ fl oz) of cocktail bitters after a large meal one of the most effective ways to aid digestion.

GARDEN ANGELICA (ANGELICA ARCHANGELICA)

The garden angelica, or wild celery, is essentially a pumped-up carrot or celery, if you like. Along with carrots, parsley and celery, it is classified in the *Apiaceae* plant family, which, more helpfully, used to be called the *Umbelliferae* after the umbrella-shaped arrangement of their tiny flowers. I remember the garden angelica well from my time in London, where it has grown wild beside the River Thames since at least the late nineteenth century (and, in deliberate cultivation nearby, in Kew Gardens, since 1768). The herbalist John Gerard, advised in 1633 that 'the root is available against witchcraft and enchantments, if a man carry the same'. Its wild relative in London, *Angelica sylvestris*, can reach 2.5 m (8 ft) tall in flower, but has been largely displaced from urban riverbanks.

IRIS (IRIS FLORENTINA)

One of Gilles' favourite botanicals. You should see him swoon when we make the tincture. When used in alcohol production, the dried root of the iris, known as orris root, is used as a fixative, meaning it helps to hold the oils and water together in the blend of botanicals and wine. It is also used extensively in the gin-making industry alongside angelica root for its similar fixative properties. It is named after the Greek goddess of the rainbow and its inner petals are considered to represent faith, wisdom and valour. Such a romantic history and, if that isn't enough, it's a beautiful plant too with around 300 species, most of which are easy to grow.

barks

Barks act similarly to roots in bringing some bitter notes to vermouth.

They are incredibly aromatic, too. Many barks have antiseptic properties, which is to say, next time you cut yourself, skimp on the antiseptic cream and drink some vermouth instead.

CINNAMON RUB

This recipe is similar to a Jamaican jerk rub, but with more cinnamon and a little coffee thrown into the mix. It is great rubbed on any meat, but is especially good on pork and chicken.

MAKES 80 G (2¾ OZ)

50 g (1¾ oz) **light brown sugar**

10 g (¼ oz) **ground cinnamon**

10 g (¼ oz) **freshly ground coffee beans**

5 g (⅛ oz) **chilli flakes**

pinch of ground nutmeg

5 g (⅛ oz) **ground cloves**

Combine all the ingredients in a bowl and mix well.

Rub the spice mix all over your choice of meat 30 minutes before grilling over an open flame.

CINNAMON (CINNAMOMUM VERUM, C. CASSIA)

To meet the eighteenth century culinary demand for this spice in Europe, Spain established huge plantations of *Cinnamomum* in Central America – nearly half a million trees in total. They understood that this tropical to subtropical genus would struggle to survive around the Mediterranean. Today, there are two species grown commonly for their aromatic bark: *Cinnamomum cassia*, producing cassia bark, and *Cinnamomum verum*, 'true cinnamon'. While cassia bark holds its flavour better during cooking, it is reputedly more bitter and of inferior flavour than true cinnamon. Here in Australia, the best-known cinnamon is Camphor Laurel, *Cinnamomum camphora*, a popular street tree in Melbourne and much-despised weed in northern Australia. Camphor oil is distilled from the bark and wood, or may be inhaled directly after trees have been freshly lopped.

CINCHONA (CINCHONA CALISAYA, C. SUCCIRUBRA)

Cinchona bark is obtained from several species of *Cinchona*, the famous plant source of antimalarial quinine, a drug whose influence on the world of medicine has been compared to the influence of gunpowder on warfare. A subsection of aromatised wines called quinquinas must use this malaria-fighting bark to classify as a quinquina. Cinchona is also the main botanical in tonic water, which, if you think about it, is the vermouth of the soft-drink world. My favourite story about cinchona has to be around the discovery of its antimalarial properties. It is said that the Countess of Cinchona contracted malaria in Peru and the natives convinced her to bathe in a pond of water made bitter by nearby cinchona trees. She bathed and she was cured, hallelujah! This has since been disproved by historians, but you should never let the truth get in the way of a good story.

CORK (QUERCUS SUBER)

Cork, or *suber* in Latin, is part of the *Quercus* (Oak) family. This medium-sized evergreen tree is native to south-west Europe and north-west North Africa and has a broad-spreading canopy. It grows in open woodland areas with cold, moist winters and dry, hot summers, generally in acidic soils on hillsides and lower slopes. The National Arboretum in Canberra has a plantation dating back to around 1920. About 2,600 trees have survived from the original plantation, and many have been harvested for their cork for use in interior design, shoemaking and soundproofing, but not for making wine corks. Most wine cork production is concentrated in Portugal, Spain and around the Mediterranean Sea. While not directly used as a botanical or flavouring, cork still plays a vital role in the bottling of vermouth, so we have included it here.

flowers

There are many usable parts of a flower. Rose petals, for example, can be used in skincare products and in cooking, whereas saffron, the vivid stigma of a *Crocus sativus*, is a highly-prized spice.

No matter what part of the plant they are from, these aromatics all make you feel as if you are walking through a garden on a warm summer evening. A vermouth without flowers is like a dish without seasoning; you can still get it down but it will taste very bland.

MANZANILLA
MANZANILLA

Or, Chamomile Fino. Whatever you decide to call it, it's delightful. Drink it chilled au naturale as an aperitif or, for the more adventurous, add half a measure to a gin and tonic.

MAKES 405 ML (13½ FL OZ)

1 × 375 ml (12½ fl oz) bottle fino sherry, chilled
4 tablespoons dried chamomile flowers, such as chamomile tea
30 ml (1 fl oz) 2:1 Sugar Syrup (page 77)

Combine all the ingredients in a bowl and leave to macerate for 30 minutes, stirring occasionally.

Strain the sherry through a fine-mesh sieve into a jug, discarding the flowers. Pour the infused sherry into a sterilised glass bottle or jar (see page 78) and store the Manzanilla Manzanilla in the refrigerator for up to 2 weeks.

CHAMOMILE (CHAMAEMELUM NOBILE)

Just add hot water and you have a lovely libation that will lull you off to sleep. Chamomile is a beautifully complex botanical, showing off delicate floral aromatics, hints of apple, and a lingering earthiness. In Spain, chamomile is known as *manzanilla*, which is curious as Manzanilla is also a variety of fino sherry, a fortified wine produced in southern Spain. Perhaps it is serendipitous that these items share a name as they taste great when combined in a little aperitif. Chamomile is also a key botanical in Tanqueray No. 10 gin.

CLOVE (SYZYGIUM AROMATICUM)

The clove is the 6-month-old flower bud of a lilly-pilly relative from Indonesia, called *Syzygium aromaticum*. The genus name refers to leaves being opposite each other on the stem – as they are in all lilly-pillies – and the species name celebrates its exotic aroma. That aroma made cloves big business in the fifteenth century, helping traders such as the Dutch East India Company make their fortune. The dried flower buds were used as a spice, a food preservative and in medicine. Although you can grow clove trees outdoors in many parts of southern Australia, they may not produce flowers, or indeed the more sought-after flower buds.

SAFFRON (CROCUS SATIVUS)

Famously known as the world's most expensive spice, it takes around 150,000 plants and 400 hours of work just to produce a measly 1 kg (2 lb 3 oz) of saffron! This is because saffron is made up of three tiny stigmas that grow inside the flower. Saffron has a range of uses, from Chinese medicine to food dye and in many world cuisines. French *bouillabaisse* and Spanish *paella* both call for saffron, where a small amount is used to great effect. In the liquor world, Fernet-Branca uses a tremendous amount of saffron to achieve its famous orange colour.

fruits

Fruits, in the botanical world, aren't just for snacks at school recess.

To vermouth, they add a perception of sweetness even if no sugar has been added. Vanilla, for example, is considered to have a sweet smell, but in its raw form, it is anything but.

CITRUS SHERBET

This is a great cordial-like product that has a number of uses, from making cocktails to forming the base of the best home-made lemonade in the world. You start by making an *oleo-saccharum*, or sugar oil, then dissolving that into the pressed juice from the fruit. It can be made with any citrus, although my personal favourite for this sherbet is red grapefruit, and it is used to make Squeeze The Americano (page 138).

MAKES APPROX. 1–1.2 LITRES (34–41 FL OZ)

6 red grapefruits, or other citrus fruit of your choice

caster (superfine) **sugar, for sweetening**

Zest the grapefruits into a bowl. Halve and juice the fruit and pour the juice into a jug. For every 1 ml ($\frac{1}{10}$ fl oz) of juice add 1 g ($\frac{1}{10}$ oz) of sugar to the zest and leave the bowl in a warm place for 3 hours to macerate.

Add the juice to the sugar mixture and stir to dissolve the sugar. Strain through a fine-mesh sieve into a sterilised glass jar or bottle (see page 78), seal tightly and store in the refrigerator for up to 1 week.

For a lovely citrus lemonade, mix 1 part sherbet with 3 parts soda water (club soda) or sparkling water for a lovely citrus lemonade, or use the sherbet as an ingredient in cocktails.

CITRUS (CITRUS AURANTIUM, C. LIMON, C. RETICULATA)

It's amazing to think that the wide variety of citrus available today is believed to have developed from as little as three original varieties, or five, depending on which botanist you speak to. Different citrus varieties work well with different types of booze. Perhaps the most famous combinations of citrus and alcohol are Limoncello, the Italian lemon liqueur, and various orange liqueurs, such as Cointreau or Grand Marnier. Bitter orange plays a huge role in a lot of vermouths, as does lemon. Blood orange is used in liqueurs such as Solerno and Amaro, lime is a key ingredient in the cocktail ingredient Falernum, and grapefruit finds its way into gins such as Melbourne Gin Company and Tanqueray No. 10. Further afield, yuzu is combined with sake to make a sweet-flavoured Japanese drink called *yuzushu*. The list of citrus-and-booze combinations is long, and it demonstrates how important citrus is in the world of liquor.

VANILLA (VANILLA PLANIFOLIA)

The world's second most expensive spice behind saffron owes its high price, in part, to its lengthy production process. There are only a couple of natural pollinators for *Vanilla planifolia*, including bees in the *Eulaema* genus and hummingbirds, and they have a very small success rate. Because of this, pollination must be done by hand and the window to do so is very short – around 12 hours – during the flowering phase. It then takes up to 9 months for the fruit to ripen, after which time it is picked and undergoes a process of fermentation and drying that takes up to another 6 months. All of this effort is certainly reflected in the price, and it is not uncommon to see vanilla priced at AUD$1,000 per kilo. Carpano Antica Formula uses a significant amount of vanilla, which brings beautiful warmth and depth to the vermouth, along with its sweetness.

JUNIPER (JUNIPERUS COMMUNIS)

Juniper is a type of conifer tree that is grown throughout Europe and forms the main ingredient of an entire drinks category – gin. Generally wild-grown, juniper is a slow-growing tree with a slow-ripening berry that resembles a small cone. It is highly aromatic and flavoursome and ideal for distillation or maceration due to its high a-Pinene and myrcene content. Aromas and flavours can vary, from the lighter pine needle with lemon thyme characteristics, through to resinous pine oil with rosemary characteristics. Much of this variation depends on how the juniper is treated by distillers and explains the vast array of gin styles.

leaves

Leaves are an important component of all plants.

They harness the power of the sun to make food for the plant with an action called photosynthesis. Science aside, the leaves of plants can be incredibly pungent and quite 'green' in flavour, adding an extra layer of freshness to a recipe.

MEDITERRANEAN TINCTURE

A tincture is an alcoholic extraction of flavour from a botanical, in this case four traditional botanicals used in Mediterranean cuisine: rosemary, thyme, parsley and sage. This liquid extraction can be added to your Bloody Mary or gin and tonic – even to your Martini. It is also great for adding to sauces, dressings and olive oil.

MAKES 100 ML (3½ FL OZ)

5 g (¼ oz) **fresh rosemary leaves, chopped**

5 g (¼ oz) **fresh sage leaves, chopped**

5 g (¼ oz) **fresh thyme leaves, chopped**

5 g (¼ oz) **fresh flat-leaf** (Italian) **parsley leaves, chopped**

1 × 100 ml (3½ fl oz) **bottle of rectified spirit** (95% ABV)

Combine all the ingredients in an airtight container and leave in a cool, dark place for 2 days to macerate. Strain the herbs through a fine-mesh sieve into a sterilised glass gar or bottle (see page 78) and store in the refrigerator for up to 2 months.

Use to enhance your beverages with Mediterranean flavours, but remember that a little goes a long way.

COMMON THYME (THYMUS VULGARIS)

Common Thyme is a member of the mint family, *Lamiaceae*, along with its partners in song, sage and rosemary (but not parsley). This family is also where you'll find our native Australian mint, *Prostanthera rotundifolia*, a flavouring in some local vermouths. There are a few species, and plenty of cultivars, of thyme available for seasoning food and drink. *Thymus vulgaris*, like most thyme species, is native to the Mediterranean region or nearby, but the genus extends to Greenland and into Asia. Nearly all are small shrubs with wiry stems and aromatic leaves, which are at their most pungent just before flowering.

COMMON ROSEMARY (ROSMARINUS OFFICINALIS)

Rosemary has got to be one of the most well-known herbs. It's delightful in cooking and super easy to grow in the garden. Medicinally, rosemary is used to treat poor circulation, migraines, depression, exhaustion, anxiety, menstrual pain and loss of appetite. Externally, it can be used to treat ailments ranging from arthritis and wounds, to dandruff and even hair loss. Common Rosemary is not so common; more like superstar rosemary, in my humble opinion.

COMMON SAGE (SALVIA OFFICINALIS)

This garden plant has a history that is far from common. The genus name is from the Latin word *salvere*, meaning 'to be well'. Throughout history, it has been used to ward off evil, fight the plague, increase longevity and enhance fertility. Sage has also been known as a recreational drug when taken in high doses. It contains camphoraceous oil, which is about 50 per cent thujone, a compound that is said to bring on hallucinations. Thujone is also a compound in wormwood, the ingredient in absinthe that gave it such a bad rap all those years ago.

seeds

Seeds are used in the production of vermouth for one very simple reason: spice.

They bring a lovely warming characteristic that often reminds me of mulled wine and apple pie. Seeds are quite often dried to intensify their flavour so, generally speaking, a little goes a long way.

CUMIN, CORIANDER & FENNEL TEA

This tea is touted to help with weight loss, supposedly stimulating digestion, which sounds great. The only problem is, it doesn't taste very good. But, with the addition of maple syrup (which probably eclipses the alleged health-giving properties), this tea becomes an absolute delight. Enjoy a cup on a cold winter afternoon after a late lunch.

SERVES 1

½ teaspoon cumin seeds
1 teaspoon fennel seeds
1 teaspoon coriander seeds
15 ml (½ fl oz) **maple syrup**

Infuse all the ingredients in 200 ml (7 fl oz) hot water for 5 minutes, then strain through a tea strainer and drink.

CORIANDER (CORIANDRUM SATIVUM)

The seeds, not the leaves, of coriander are used in vermouth, so we can ignore the alternate name for the leafy parts, cilantro. We can also put to one side the fact that people tend to love or hate the taste of the leaves – the genus name comes from the word *coris*, Greek for 'bugs', and alludes to the smell of the crushed plant. Obtusely, a chemical within coriander acts as an 'odour-eating agent', working at concentrations of 10 parts per billion (about 10 drops per Olympic-size swimming pool) to neutralise strong-smelling foods such as chitterlings (hog intestines eaten for Thanksgiving in the southern Unites States). The seeds, or, more correctly, the dried fruits, have different active chemicals and flowers, thank goodness. One of the most interesting ways that coriander acts as a botanical interacting with alcohol is that it gives a strong perception of citrus flavour. When distilled or macerated, coriander comes across as an almost hot or spiced-lemon characteristic, lending beautiful citrus notes to vermouth and gin. There are only two species of *Coriandrum*, with the widely-cultivated *Coriandrum sativum* apparently native from the eastern Mediterranean through to south-west Asia.

NUTMEG (MYRISTICA FRAGRANS)

Nutmeg, believe it or not, can be quite toxic. There are actual accounts of people getting nutmeg poisoning from consuming too much: as little as 2 tablespoons. The reason people overdose on it is because of the active ingredient, called myristicin, which is believed to have psychoactive properties. However, doctors report that people suffering from nutmeg poisoning experience more nausea than out-of-body experiences. Grated nutmeg was traditionally used in punches, so much so that exquisite antique nutmeg grating boxes were all the rage in the 1600s: a must-have item for the punch aficionado.

CARDAMOM (ELETTARIA CARDAMOMUM)

There are two common types of cardamom used in food and drinks: green and black. The more common green cardamom has strong ties to Indian cuisine and gives dishes a resinous aromatic flavour. Black cardamom is a little smokier in comparison. The green variety is used quite a lot in gin production as it has the ability, similar to vanilla, to give the appearance of sweetness without actually adding any sugar, as well as providing an aromatic lift to the spirit. It also pairs incredibly well with citrus fruits, accentuating their flavours.

NATIVE AUSTRALIAN BOTANICALS

Australia, the lucky country, really is lucky when it comes to unique vegetation, due mostly to its geographical isolation, which has allowed plants to evolve without interference.

We still know so little about our native plants in comparison to other countries but, despite this, using native ingredients is very much in vogue in high-end restaurants in Australia, and this is slowly filtering down to more mainstream establishments too. Demand for these ingredients, popularised by the likes of Attica in Melbourne, and high-profile culinary pop-ups like Noma, is currently outstripping the supply. At Maidenii, we use native Australian botanicals in our vermouth as it helps to evoke a sense of place. That, and there are some amazing flavours that are distinctively Australian.

*from the
land of the
contrarieties*

WATTLE

(ACACIA)

Wattles in Australia are species of *Acacia*, or, rarely, and mostly in the north, *Senegalia* or *Vachellia*. The seeds of most of the 1,000 or so species of wattle in Australia are edible but some are definitely poisonous. We tend to stick to those we know to be safe, like the Black Wattle (*A. mearnsii*) and Blackwood (*A. melanoxylon*). The majority of the world's 1,500 wattles are native to Australia but in Africa, the thorny trees now called *Vachellia* (and once part of a broader *Acacia* concept) dominate vast areas of landscape across the continent. Wattles, whether in Africa, Asia, South America or Australia, have either leaflets in two rows like a feather or fern, or a flat blade called a phyllode – an expanded leaf stalk rather than a true leaf (such plants may have feather-like leaves when very young).

We use the roasted seeds of our national floral emblem in our core range of vermouths. I would go so far as to say we champion this botanical. Once roasted, the seeds give off an aroma of all things coffee and cacao, with a distinct nutty element. It is spectacular in gin and softens the texture in the final distillate. The West Winds gin and Ironbark gin also use this unique botanical. Wattleseed can also be used as a substitute for ground coffee in a number of food and drink recipes and actually makes a delightful caffeine-free coffee substitute. One of the best wattleseed dishes I have come across is roasted wattleseed-infused crème anglaise poured over caramelised bananas, which Nick Tesar prepared for me during a cocktail-tasting session we had a few years back.

WATTLESEED SYRUP

This syrup can be used for just about anything. Spice up your coffee with it, pour it over ice cream or use it in cocktails as a substitute for coffee liqueur. In fact, it makes an excellent Espresso Martini.

MAKES APPROX. 400 ML (13½ FL OZ)

50 g (1¾ oz) **roasted wattleseeds**

250 g (9 oz) **caster** (superfine) **sugar**

Put the wattleseeds in a saucepan with 500 ml (17 fl oz) water and set over medium heat. Simmer for 15 minutes, then strain through a fine-mesh sieve into a clean saucepan and add the sugar. Stir until dissolved, then pour the wattleseed syrup into a sterilised glass jar or bottle (see page 78), seal tightly and store in the refrigerator for up to 1 week.

SEA PARSLEY

(APIUM PROSTRATUM)

Yes it's a parsley, of sorts. Botanically we call it *A. prostratum*, a rather low-growing species from southern Australia that is one of three species in the genus that gives us celery and celeriac. As you've no doubt guessed, it also grows primarily by the sea, on sand dunes and nearby cliff faces. There are a couple of 'subspecies' and varieties but there is not much in it – mostly variations in leaf size. Along with garden angelica (see page 49), this is a member of the mostly edible *Apiaceae* family; watch out for the hemlock (*Conium maculatum*), though, and a few other highly poisonous relatives.

Also known as 'sea celery', this botanical is exceptional in soups, where it gives the characteristics of both celery and parsley. We use it in its dried form in our core vermouth range as it gives earthy, almost tobacco-like aromas to the vermouth. The West Winds also use it in their Broadside gin in addition to sea salt and it's terrific. Serve this gin in a gin and tonic with a touch of fino sherry.

BROADSIDE G&T

This G&T is meatier than most, with a little dash of fino sherry to emphasise the salty characteristics of the sea parsley. 'd suggest a Manzanilla, which s a little saltier than regular ino, and you don't need to dd much: about one-third of he amount of gin you would ormally use.

SERVES 1

30 ml (1 fl oz) **West Winds Broadside gin**

10 ml (¼ fl oz) **fino sherry**

90 ml (3 fl oz) **tonic water**

ice cubes

sea parsley or a lemon wedge, to garnish (optional)

Build all the ingredients except the sea parsley over ice in a highball glass. Garnish with sea parsley or a lemon wedge, if using.

STRAWBERRY GUM

(EUCALYPTUS OLIDA)

Strawberry gum is a medium-sized tree (approximately 20 m/65 ft tall) that grows mainly around New South Wales. Its long aromatic leaves have an intense berry aroma and flavour with hints of eucalypt. As a bush medicine, Indigenous Australians chewed the leaves for their unique berry flavour and put wet branches over a fire to create steam and release the aroma, which was thought to help with nausea. Strawberry gum leaves have been used in the confectionery, baking and cosmetics industries, and are now widely used by Australian chefs and the distilling industry.

Strawberry gum is one of our favourite botanicals. We use quite a bit of it in our sweet vermouth production. The strawberry component comes from a chemical called methyl cinnamate, which is also found in strawberries. Besides us, Poor Toms use it quite extensively in their gin, as do Brocken Spectre in theirs. A really simple way to enjoy strawberry gum across a range of desserts is to make a strawberry gum icing sugar, which you can then use as a substitute in any recipe that calls for icing (confectioners') sugar to give the dish a zing of strawberry gum.

STRAWBERRY GUM ICING SUGAR

Flavoured sugars are great for finishing desserts and cakes, and this one has a uniquely Australian twist.

MAKES 100 G (3½ OZ)

100 g (3½ oz) **icing** (confectioners') **sugar**
5 g (⅛ oz) **dried strawberry gum leaves**

Combine the sugar and gum leaves in an airtight container and leave in a cool, dark place for 2 days. Sift the icing sugar into a clean airtight container and discard the gum leaves. Seal tightly and store at room temperature for up to 2 months.

RIVER MINT

(MENTHA AUSTRALIS)

This rambling bush grows near riverbanks or in any moist conditions across the south-east of Australia. It has a beautiful small mauve flower and is popular as a ground cover in Australian gardens. The small delicate leaves have an intense spearmint flavour and aroma, and were used extensively by the early settlers for their herbal qualities and to flavour their roast lamb. As well as a food flavouring, Indigenous Australians have used these fragrant leaves in bush medicine for centuries to treat ailments ranging from coughs and colds to stomach upsets.

River mint is very similar in flavour and aroma to common garden mint, just not as intense. We use it in our vermouth to add freshness to the blend and to help balance out the spicier notes. Archie Rose and Botanic Australia also use it in the production of their gins.

MOJITO AMERICANO

Taking inspiration from the classic rum-based drink, I have swapped the rum for Cocchi Americano in this recipe. If you can't get hold of fresh river mint, fear not, common garden mint will work just as well.

SERVES 1

60 ml (2 fl oz) **Cocchi Americano**
20 ml (¾ fl oz) **lime juice**
5 ml (⅛ fl oz) **2:1 Sugar Syrup** (page 77)
ice cubes
handful of fresh river mint, plus extra to garnish

Build all the ingredients in a highball glass over ice. Garnish with extra river mint.

LEMON GUM

(CORYMBIA CITRIODORA)

This tall tree grows in the temperate and tropical north-east of Australia and can grow up to 35 m (115 ft). Also known as Lemon-scented gum, Blue-spotted gum and Lemon eucalyptus, this large forest tree is primarily harvested for structural timber and its beautiful lemon-scented leaves. The essential oil from the leaves is ideal for perfumes and is becoming popular in the Australian bush-food industry. For centuries, Indigenous Australians have utilised lemon gum as an insect repellent by crushing the leaves to release their powerful aromas.

A very interesting botanical that, as you can probably tell from its common name, shows aromas of eucalyptus and lemon. Local Australian gin-makers, Anther, use it to bring a unique freshness to their botanical blend, as do we in the production of our quinquina. It makes an excellent cordial and the perfect summer's day drink when mixed with sparkling water and lots of ice.

LEMON GUM CORDIAL

This cordial makes an excellent spritz for the summer, but it's also great in a Gin Hot Toddy. Simply mix 1 part cordial with 1 part Anther gin and 4 parts hot water and drop in a lemon wedge. Delightful on a chilly autumn evening.

MAKES 650 ML (22 FL OZ)

650 g (1 lb 7 oz) **caster** (superfine) **sugar**

20 g (¾ oz) **fresh lemon gum leaves** (crushed in your hands)

10 g (¼ oz) **citric acid**

Combine all the ingredients in a saucepan with 650 ml (22 fl oz) water and bring to the boil over medium–high heat. Reduce the heat to medium and simmer for 30 minutes, then remove from the heat and leave to cool.

Strain the cordial through a fine-mesh sieve into a sterilised glass jar or bottle (see page 78) and store in the refrigerator for up to 2 weeks.

DAVIDSON PLUM

(DAVIDSONIA)

There are several species of these tart, edible bush-fruit trees growing in the subtropical and tropical areas of Australia, from northern New South Wales to Queensland. The fruit grows in large clusters on the trunk of the tree and very closely resembles the English bloom plum, despite not being related. They are a great source of potassium, lutein for eye health, vitamin E, folate, zinc, magnesium and calcium. Because of the intense sour flavour, the fruit is best used in cooking and distilling rather than being eaten as a fresh fruit.

I was first introduced to Davidson plum while working at Gin Palace. I thought it would make an excellent substitute for sloe berries in sloe gin. We made one and it was quite nice. A few years later a buddy of mine, Eddie Brook, took the concept one step further and made an amazing product by macerating Davidson plums in his Brookie's Byron Bay dry gin. We also use Davidson plum in our Maidenii Nocturne, which combines all the warm flavours of plum with high levels of acidity to help balance the sweetness.

SPIKED HOT CHOCOLATE

Another one for the cooler months, I would highly recommend enjoying this hot chocolate with some toasted marshmallows by an open fire.

SERVES 1

Simply make a hot chocolate using your favourite recipe and add a small (or large) measure of Brookie's Slow gin; easy and delicious.

FINGER LIME

(CITRUS AUSTRALASICA)

Most people are surprised to learn that about half of the world's 25 species of *Citrus* come from Australia, Papua New Guinea or New Caledonia. This includes the finger lime, *Citrus australasica*, which is the parent of many of the new cultivars bred by the CSIRO and others. One example is the Australian Blood lime, a hybrid between a red-fruited variety of finger lime and a Rangpur lime, itself a cross between a mandarin and a lemon, and probably grafted onto Hardy Orange, or *Citrus trifoliata*, stock from China. Another popular cultivar is Australian Sunrise, a cross between a (non-red) variety of finger lime and a Calamondin, which is a mandarin crossed with a cumquat. And so on, with plenty more to come I expect.

My first experience using finger limes in booze was with Four Pillars gin at Gin Palace. The gin-makers wanted to develop their Navy Strength gin and we were the testing and feedback bar. Initially, Navy Strength began as their regular gin at a higher proof, but over the testing period new botanicals were added and the finger lime really started to hit its stride. Finger limes are great in distilling as they work really well with juniper, the predominant botanical in many gins. (Remember, if it doesn't contain juniper, it ain't gin.) The combination was fantastic, with citrus notes and hints of anise. We use finger lime for exactly the same reason in our quinquina; it really lifts and holds up some of the spicier botanicals. A must-try is to rim a cocktail glass with finger lime 'caviar', then pour in a margarita – delightful!

OYSTERS WITH FINGER LIME

This is one of my favourite ways to enjoy oysters.

Simply shuck as many oysters as you like and squeeze some finger lime 'caviar' on top. No recipe needed, just some dry vermouth to sip on the side.

RIBERRY

(SYZYGIUM LUEHMANNII)

Syzygium luehmannii was described by Ferdinand von Mueller in 1893, from a specimen collected for him from the tallest peak in Queensland, Mount Bartle Frere. It's a small-leaved lilly-pilly with bright red fruit tasting of nutmeg, bay leaf and cloves – in fact, it is sometimes called the Clove Lilly-Pilly. Mueller called it a *Eugenia*, which was where it sat until 1962 when the then Director of Sydney's Royal Botanic Garden, Lawrie Johnson, moved it into *Syzygium* at the time of a major revision of the lilly-pillies. There are lots of other lilly-pillies with colourful and tasty fruits that might add complexity to a vermouth. Look for the genera *Eugenia*, *Acmena* and of course *Syzygium*.

Such a strong-flavoured botanical that has surprisingly spicy characteristics in spite of its appearance, and it gives off heady aromas of clove and anise. In Australia, Okar Amaro is well known for using riberries to give their product its signature red colour and much of its flavour. Story gin also use a significant amount in their botanical blend and we use it in the production of our Maidenii Nocturne.

SPIKED LAPSANG SOUCHONG

The smoky, tannic flavours of lapsang souchong tea work incredibly well with the spicy notes of Okar Amaro.

SERVES 1

Brew a cup of tea using lapsang souchong leaves and add a small measure of Okar. You don't need much; 10 ml (¼ fl oz) per 200 ml (7 fl oz) of tea should be sufficient.

MUNTRIE

(KUNZEA POMIFERA)

This native berry bush grows in the south-east of South Australia and western Victoria. In its natural state, it is a low-growing ground cover, but is often trellised for commercial purposes. The bush has small round leaves with a profusion of feathery cream flowers in spring. The small fruit are green to red with a purplish tinge when ripe and packed full of vitamin C and antioxidants – significantly higher than blueberries – and can be eaten fresh. They are extremely popular in the food and beverage industries for their sweet, spicy, apple-juniper flavour.

Whenever I think of muntries I think of apple pie. All the flavours of an apple pie are in the muntrie fruit: apple, cinnamon, vanilla and even a hint of clove. We use it quite heavily in Maidenii Nocturne, as do many gin distilleries. While working at Lûmé, Nick Tesar used them glacéed and added them to Umeshu, a Japanese liqueur. It was a match made in heaven.

MUNTRIE JAM

Making this jam is a really good way to harness the flavour of muntries and be able to use it all year round. Quite a bit of sugar is needed to bring out the flavour, but it is worth it. Smother the jam on slices of toasted brioche and, if you're feeling fancy, drizzle over some crème anglaise. Alternatively, try it out in cocktails such as Kunzea Pomifera (page 124).

MAKES APPROX. 800 G (1 LB 12 OZ)

500 g (1 lb 2 oz) **muntries**
500 g (1 lb 2 oz) **caster** (superfine) **sugar**
50 ml (1¾ fl oz) **fresh lemon juice**

Combine all the ingredients in a large, heavy-based saucepan with 250 ml (8½ fl oz) water and stir to combine. Bring to the boil over medium–high heat, then reduce the heat to low and simmer for 1 hour.

Remove from the heat then carefully blend the jam with a hand-held blender until well combined. Transfer to a sterilised glass jar (see page 78), seal tightly and store in the refrigerator for up to 2 months.

MACADAMIA

(MACADAMIA INTEGRIFOLIA, M. TETRAPHYLLA)

The world's first cultivated macadamia, *Macadamia integrifolia*, still grows in the City Botanic Gardens in Brisbane. It was planted in 1858 by Walter Hill, superintendent of the gardens, a year after Ferdinand von Mueller described this plant, honouring a chemist from Melbourne, John Macadam. Yet, despite this, and despite it being harvested and eaten by Indigenous communities in south-east Queensland, macadamia was commercialised first in Hawaii, in 1882. Australian production began in 1963. *Macadamia integrifolia* has leaves in whorls of three while the other species grown commercially for nut production, *Macadamia tetraphylla*, has leaves in groups of four.

Perhaps the most well known and widely exported Australian native, there are significant plantations of macadamia in Hawaii and South Africa, as well as various parts of Australia. My first experience with macadamias in booze was when my friend Andrew Marks launched the Melbourne Gin Company. The use of macadamia in distilling works similarly to almonds, by giving softness and texture to the distillate. And boy does it give great texture! Pick up a bottle of Melbourne Gin Company gin and try it for yourself. Almonds can also be substituted for macadamias in the production of orgeat, a staple cocktail syrup usually made with almonds.

MACADAMIA BRITTLE

The first cocktail I developed with Maidenii after its launch was Summer's Funeral (page 128). We served it at Gin Palace with this brittle on the side. It goes really well with the cocktail, but is equally good on its own, perhaps served after dinner with something sweet. Chinato, anyone?

MAKES 1.2–1.5 KG (2 LB 10 OZ–3 LB 5 OZ)

150 g (5½ oz) **salted butter, cubed, plus extra for greasing**
300 g (10½ oz) **macadamia nuts, roughly chopped**
1 kg (2 lb 3 oz) **caster** (superfine) **sugar**
250 ml (8½ fl oz) **Maidenii Classic vermouth**
250 ml (8½ fl oz) **cloudy apple juice**

Grease a baking tray and spread the chopped nuts on top.

Combine the sugar, vermouth and apple juice in a saucepan and bring to the boil over medium–high heat. Boil for 15 minutes, without stirring, until the sugar has dissolved. Brush any sugar crystals from the side of the pan into the caramel with a pastry brush.

Once the caramel turns a deep golden colour, quickly whisk in the butter and carefully pour the mixture over the macadamia nuts. Leave to set at room temperature for 3 hours before eating (if you can wait that long).

how
to
drink

BAR JARGON

(AND BASIC RECIPES)

In this chapter, I aim to throw some light on mystical bartending terminology and arm you with the basic techniques, tips and recipes you will need to take your cocktail game to the next level.

As a failsafe, I'd like to include my email address, in case you are having trouble or don't fully understand something: shaun@maidenii.com.au. I'll be more than happy to help.

RECIPES

There are several fundamental recipes that every cocktail maker should have in their arsenal. The ones below pop up frequently in this book, so take a moment to familiarise yourself with the basics.

CITRIC SOLUTION

When I first started making cocktails, it was drilled into me that you need to consider three things: the sweet, the sour and the bitter. Often, the sour element comes from lemon or lime juice, but you needn't always use fresh citrus to achieve a sour flavour. Citric solution is a great alternative, and something we use all the time in the bartending trade. To make it, all you need to do is mix citric acid with water. Just remember to use 20 per cent by weight of citric acid to every 100 ml (3½ fl oz) of water, e.g. 20 g (¾ oz) citric acid to 100 ml (3½ fl oz) water.

Other solutions include tartaric acid (from grapes) and malic acid (from apples).

HONEY SYRUP

I find the flavour variation between different honeys incredible. The location and variety of plants really shapes the way a honey will taste. As a general rule, I try to balance the strength of the honey with the strength of the cocktail. A bolshy whisky and amaro number will stand up to a rich honey, while a light gin and citrus drink works better with a gentle, floral honey. The best way to get honey into a cocktail is to turn it into a syrup by mixing equal parts honey and cold water. Give it a good shake to mix and you're ready to go.

SALINE SOLUTION

If we had to turn our sweet-sour-bitter triangle into another shape, it would be a square, with the addition of salt.

It's almost amusing that, until recently, salt was excluded from the bartender's repertoire, as it really helps to enhance flavour. You might assume that adding salt to a drink will make it taste, well, salty. But that's where the magic happens. In fact, it makes drinks appear softer and fruitier, whereas drinks left unsalted appear more bitter and intense. It really is a must for anyone who likes to mix drinks. As friend of mine James Connolly says when judging new cocktails that aren't quite right: 'Have you tried adding more salt?' Without a doubt, it usually improves the outcome.

To make a saline solution, dissolve 20 per cent by weight of good-quality sea salt flakes in every 100 ml (3½ fl oz) of water, e.g. 20 g (¾ oz) sea salt flakes to 100 ml (3½ fl oz) water. Store it in the fridge and add it, drop by drop, to cocktails until you get the flavour just right.

SUGAR SYRUP

This is a bartending staple that is frequently called for in not only this, but every other, cocktail book. It is usually made with equal parts sugar and water, but I like to make it (as do many others) with 2 parts sugar to 1 part water. I prefer it for two reasons: first, the sugar helps to preserve the syrup in the fridge (I often add a shot of vodka as well to help with that), and, second, you don't end up diluting your cocktail with extra water. Water is only used as the conduit, so the less the better!

To make a 2:1 sugar syrup, combine 2 parts sugar and 1 part water in a saucepan. Heat gently over low heat until the sugar has dissolved, then pour it into a squeezy bottle and store it in the fridge for up to 2 weeks.

GLASSWARE

RINSING GLASSWARE

Rinsing glasses is designed to add an essence or aroma to a drink. Smell is an important factor in bringing a cocktail together, and this is a great way to incorporate whiffs of other ingredients. Commonly, stronger products such as absinthe or Chartreuse are used as these aromas tend to linger longer on a glass.

To rinse a glass, pour 5–10 ml (⅛–¼ fl oz) of your chosen drink into a glass and swirl to coat. Fill with ice cubes and set it aside while you prepare the rest of the cocktail. Just before pouring, discard the watery contents and you will be left with a perfectly rinsed (and also chilled) glass.

STERILISING BOTTLES & JARS

Many of the recipes in this book make shrubs, flavoured spirits and other nice things you can keep in bottles or jars and store to use in other cocktails. To keep them tasting fresh and free of any contaminants, it's important to sterilise any glass bottles or jars before using them. To do this, remove any lids and thoroughly wash the bottles or jars in hot soapy water. Place the bottles or jars on a baking tray, mouths facing up, and leave in a low oven until completely dry. The lids should be boiled for 10 minutes, then left to air-dry on a clean tea towel (dish towel) until completely dry.

SELECTING YOUR GLASS

People drink with their eyes, so it's important to consider your glass selection. First, match the drink to the glass. By this, I mean make sure your glass suits the cocktail you're making. For example, I prefer to use a highball glass for a G&T – it's large enough to hold all the tonic and will keep the drink colder for longer as the thermal mass of the iced drink will have less contact with the warmer air. Plus, it looks sophisticated.

GLOSSARY

Look out for these glass symbols throughout the book.

This is a rough guide to what glass will work best with what drink, but feel free to experiment with whatever glassware you have on hand.

ABSINTHE GLASS
A thick glass with a foot, stem and bowl, usually used for serving absinthe.

BURGUNDY GLASS
A bowl-shaped glass that is said to best express the wine of Burgundy. It's also perfect for a generous spritz.

COCKTAIL
The V-shaped glass people commonly refer to as a Martini glass.

COLLINS
A larger version of a highball glass.

COUPETTE
A stemmed cocktail glass with a broad, shallow bowl. The shape is said to have been modelled on Marie Antoinette's breast – all strictly scientific, I'm sure.

HIGHBALL
A tall, thin glass that's not too large.

JULEP
Made of pewter more often than not, decadent ones can be hand-made in silver! Perfect for crushed-ice cocktails that frost over the cup, giving it a very drinkable appearance.

NICK & NORA
A small glass, almost like a sherry glass, that usually comes with beautiful etching on the outside.

OLD FASHIONED
A larger version of a rocks glass.

ROCKS
A small, stubby glass traditionally used for serving whisky and mixed drinks.

SMALL WINE GLASS
The use of this versatile glass shouldn't be restricted to just wine; it is great for cocktails too.

TEACUP
However it comes, but on a saucer please; we aren't heathens.

TULIP
A delicate piece of glassware with lovely curves, perfect for serving fortified wine and flips.

GARNISHES

Food can bring out the flavour of what you are drinking.

This is partly why sommeliers recommend different wines for different dishes. Food and wine matching is commonplace, but it needn't end there. A cocktail can be just as complex and interesting, and I'm a big believer in having something to eat alongside a drink, which might explain my expanding waistline. In this book, I've included both garnishes and accompaniments, with garnishes served in the cocktail and accompaniments on the side. Both can really help to add another dimension to drinks and lift the flavours of your ingredients.

'SPANKING' SOFT HERBS

Now, it might sound saucy, but this little bartender's secret really elevates the quality of cocktails. Put simply, 'spanking' (or bruising) soft herbs crushes their cells to release the aroma. Why this matters is a little more detailed and nerdy. When we drink a cocktail, we engage both our gustatory system (our tastebuds) and our olfactory system (our sense of smell). What we smell affects what we taste, and the first things to hit our nose when we lift up our glass are the garnishes, so choose them wisely and spank them ruthlessly (the herbs, that is).

CITRUS TWISTS

Many cocktails call for some kind of citrus twist. Before we get on to the 'how', let's discuss the 'why'. Why, that is, should you ruin a perfectly good piece of fruit just to harvest a tiny twist? It's where all the flavour and aroma is. Citrus oil is a powerful aromatic and a little bit goes a long way towards engaging the senses. Instead of rubbing the rim of your glass with citrus rind, try rubbing it on the outside of the glass and stem. This might sound weird, but you send your guests home smelling of citrus instead of the one-too-many glasses of plonk. Try it, you'll see.

The best way to prepare a twist for garnish is to peel the fruit from top to bottom with a vegetable peeler. Squeeze the twist over the top of the drink to extract the oil, then either drop it in, wedge it on the rim of the glass or discard altogether. It might make for an uglier cocktail, but I actually prefer to discard mine and let the flavours of the drink shine.

APPLE FAN

I know what you're thinking: fruit fans are so retro.
But really, isn't that all part of the fun? In fact, I find it's
one of the easiest ways to put a professional spin on your
cocktails, and you can use a variety of fruit, including
apples, pears, peaches and nectarines. No matter what
you use, they always look great.

Cut the cheek off an apple then cut it into three 1 cm
(½ in) slices. Fan them out and plant them in your
cocktail – so simple, yet so effective! Another method,
favoured by my old boss at Gin Palace, Ben Luzz, is to cut
an apple wedge, then sliced a diamond shape into the
apple skin about 1 cm (½ in) from each end. Cut towards
the middle so the two cuts join about 1 cm (½ in) from
the bottom. If successful, you'll have a wedge within a
wedge. Repeat on the next smallest wedge and see how
many wedges you can get.

FLAMING ORANGE

Naturally, the next step on from preparing a citrus
garnish is to set it on fire. It might sound like an excuse
for pyrotechnics, but it actually works to add a certain
flavour (not to mention flair) to your drinks. I first
learned about this eye-catching garnish while working
at nightclubs in the early 2000s when Cosmopolitans
were all the rage.

It's actually quite easy to execute. Simply prepare a citrus
twist (see opposite) and, while squeezing out the oils,
put a flame between the twist and cocktail. It's flashy,
for sure, and some people swear it adds a burnt citrus
flavour, but in my personal opinion it's more for show.
What it does add is theatre, fire and a certain panache to
the drink, and it's definitely memorable.

STRAWS

OK, technically not a garnish, but a very important part
of finishing a drink.

Thankfully, this subject is becoming a talking point
around the proverbial water cooler among bartenders.
Straws are used in many cocktails, but the drinks are
often let down by the cheap, plastic straws that don't do
anything to emphasise the quality of the drink. Metal
straws are a good alternative and many bars now use
them. They are recyclable, conduct cold and, frankly, look
much better if you have gone to the trouble of making
a nice drink in a nice glass. They also help to transfer
the aroma of a cocktail when used to support garnishes,
which in turn contributes to how you will taste the
drink. So, where do I stand with straws? They are great in
certain cocktails, but please, carefully consider the type
you use to pimp your drink. Hippie rant over.

Ice is often the forgotten ingredient in a cocktail. When I first started bartending, I only knew of two kinds of ice: crushed and cubed. As time wore on, things started improving and new fancy ice machines came out that produced bigger, clearer cubes.

Bars started boasting about the quality of their ice and began freezing it in bigger blocks to serve with their premium whiskies. I even heard of a bar that claimed to use the purest ice in the world, sourced from Antarctica. That may be taking it a step too far, but still, this change in attitude towards ice has brought about some great new options, not to mention a marketable ingredient.

Choosing the right kind of ice for your drink is important. It serves two essential purposes: chilling and diluting. Chilling can help round out a drink by softening harsher flavours, and dilution helps to add a small amount of water, which opens up aromas. A good example of this effect is to look at how temperature affects sweetness. A chilled drink – particularly vermouth – mutes the perception of sweetness as opposed to a drink served at room temperature. I can't explain the science, but it works.

Making different kinds of ice is a lot easier than it might seem. Fill a large plastic container with water and freeze overnight. Remove the large ice block and leave it to melt slightly on a clean tea towel (dish towel). Using a sharp knife, carve it into whatever shape; it's a bit like whittling wood. An easier way is to buy a specific freezing vessel that freezes your ice in the desired shapes. These days, you can buy individual moulds, moulds that use directional freezing to give you crystal-clear ice, and specific Japanese ice saws for cutting. If, like me, you are excited by this, look up Japanese ice carving on YouTube. You won't be sorry.

CHILLING

So you have mixed the perfect cocktail, found the right glass and shaken or stirred it like a pro. 'What next?', I hear you ask. The recipe says 'strain it into a glass, so that's what I'm going to do ...' Wait! Hold on a second! You have gone to all this effort to get your cocktail to the right temperature, so don't ruin it by pouring it into a room temperature or, worse, a warm glass. It's like cooking the perfect bolognese only to serve it over slimy, overcooked pasta.

If you're making a chilled drink with ice, be sure to chill your glass before starting preparation. This is easy: just fill your glass with ice cubes and let it sit while you mix the cocktail. Discard the ice right before you pour the drink. For hot beverages, do the same, but with hot water.

We recommend several different kinds of ice in this book:

 CUBED
Regular ice cubes from an ice-cube tray or ice machine; 2–3 cm (¾–1¼ in) is ideal.

CRUSHED
Essentially, cubed ice smashed with a rolling pin or crushed in an ice crusher for those times when only a delicate touch will do.

ROCK
A large block of ice that fits – almost perfectly – into an Old Fashioned or rocks glass.

SPEAR
A long thin block of ice designed to fit into a highball or Collins glass.

PUNCH
One really large cube of ice to fit inside a punch bowl or vessel.

YOU'VE COME THIS FAR, SO HERE ARE SOME OTHER USEFUL THINGS TO KNOW ...

JUICES

As a general rule, when juice is called for in a recipe, it is all but mandatory to use freshly squeezed juice. There aren't many things that I flatly advise against, but pasteurised, preserved and sickly-sweet juice is one of them. These products *might* be fine on their own, but when mixed in a cocktail, they just don't work. Comparing fresh and processed juice is like comparing an Aston Martin DB9 with a Smart car. It'll still run, but you're in for a bumpy ride. The bonus here is that freshly squeezed juice costs little more than the processed stuff, but it doubles – maybe even triples – the flavour and freshness. Always use fruit that is in season and feel free to play around with different citrus in your cocktails.

FRUIT PURÉES

This is a great way to pack a lot of fruit – especially berries – into your cocktails. It's really easy: just blitz the fruit in a food processor and pass the purée through a fine-mesh sieve. Transfer to a squeezy bottle and store in the fridge for up to 1 week. If you add a little sugar or a shot of vodka it will last longer but, as always, fresh is best. It's great squeezed on top of a drink to create a 'float'. The visual effect is stunning and you get an immediate hit of fruity aroma the minute you dip your nose in.

EGGS

Many cocktails call for eggs, whether that's just an egg white or the whole kit and caboodle. They are used to emulsify drinks and bring the citrus and booze together into a gloriously silky mixture. The yolk brings decadence and richness, while the white gives the kind of aeration that would put your chocolate pavlova to shame. (That's a lie, I love my mother-in-law's chocolate pav'!) If you are using eggs in your cocktails, make sure you use the best-quality, organic free-range eggs you can find. Secondly, make sure they are super fresh and always use them straight away, otherwise they will add a distinctly eggy aroma to your cocktail. Lastly, if you can't – or won't – eat eggs, there are some fine substitutes, including a product called InstaFoam, a vegan emulsifier available from onlybitters.com.au.

STRAINING

Straining is an essential function in cocktail-making. Most bartenders use a specific strainer called a Hawthorne strainer. Quite simply, it holds back ice. After shaking a beverage in a mixing glass or cocktail shaker, the strainer is used to hold back the ice while you strain your cocktail into the perfectly selected glass. The strainer's coil spring helps prevent small pieces of ice getting through, which in my opinion is really, really important. Let's take, for example, one of my favourite cocktails, the Martini. A well-made Martini is a sensuous experience, aromatically uplifting and technically flawless. The discovery of a whisper of ice in the drink is enough to ruin the whole thing so, in short, use a Hawthorne strainer if you can and even go one further by pouring first through the Hawthorne strainer and then through a tea strainer to capture any rogue bits of ice.

BRANDS

OK, so you pick up a cocktail book, you find a recipe that speaks to you, you're feeling good about it, and then all it says is 'gin'. Well, what gin do you use? They all say 'gin' on the bottle, so what's the difference? There's no hard and fast rule here, but what I will say is that different gins offer different botanical profiles. And the best gins aren't always the ones with the hefty price tags. Without doubt, one of the best on the market is also one of the cheapest: Beefeater, and I'm sure most bartenders would agree.

This goes for other spirits – and alcohols – in general, too. In this book, we have suggested the variety and/or brand that best suits the cocktail and other ingredients it will be mixed with. Where we feel strongly you should use a certain brand, it has been included. For the rest, don't despair if you cannot find the perfect unicorn hair-infused, Mordor barrel-aged whiskey; whatever you've got in the cupboard will be fine.

Unfortunately we can't try every variation of brand in a cocktail (my wife says this would just be an excuse to drink more), so you may find an even better match, and if you do, please get in touch and you can help me test the cocktails for the next book (wife permitting!).

VERMOUTH NEAT

There are many varieties of vermouth, from very dry to very sweet.

When it comes to drinking vermouth, one of the best ways to enjoy it is chilled and neat, without any ice.

WHY DRINK VERMOUTH NEAT?

When I started making vermouth, my reference point
was not aromatised wine, but sherry. It is usually drunk
neat, and my approach to drinking vermouth is the
same. Like the sherries from the Jerez region of Spain,
vermouth is best served chilled, so it is important to
keep it refrigerated. As with any other wine, temperature
changes the way we perceive a vermouth's flavours,
with colder temperatures reducing the perception of
sweetness and increasing the perception of acidity and
tannin. Served at the right temperature, without any
ice, vermouth drunk neat can shine as an aperitif and
is excellent paired with any course of a meal, as we will
discover here.

Another reason to drink vermouth neat is to heighten
the experience of the botanicals' aromatics. Just like
wine, vermouth develops in the glass. From the first
'nose' when it is initially poured, to after aeration, its
aromatic profile changes significantly, revealing different
aromas. The only way to immerse yourself in this
rich 'bouquet' is to serve vermouth on its own in the
perfect glass.

▽ IN RECENT YEARS, NEAT VERMOUTH HAS MADE
A COMEBACK AS AN APERITIF – ANDY GRIFFITHS

WHAT GLASS SHOULD I CHOOSE?

Because of vermouth's aromatic character and higher spirit content, it is best to choose a glass that is not too closed. I prefer an open tulip shape, but a tumbler would work just as well, and this is how vermouth is served in Spain.

There is a trend among glass manufacturers to create specialised glasses for different styles of wine, e.g. the Riesling glass, the Burgundy glass, etc. But, as yet, only one glass has been manufactured specifically for vermouth and it is an open stemmed glass similar to a water glass.

Stemless or stemmed? This is an interesting point. As vermouth is often used in cocktails, it finds its way into different cocktail glasses: the V-shape with a stem for a Martini; an Old Fashioned glass for a Negroni and a chimney-shaped glass for a G&T, to name a few. The use of a stemmed glass helps to keep a drink cool, whereas stemless glasses fall victim to the heat of our hands, and so, ice is required.

Prior to the 1980s, very small glasses were used for liqueurs, sweet and aromatised wines. Since then, glass dimensions have augmented in inverse proportion to the recommendations for the 'responsible service of alcohol'. Larger glasses emphasise the importance of smell when it comes to wine and vermouth, often even above its flavour. A small amount of wine in a large glass is easier to smell than a glass filled to the rim. While the shape and size of a glass is important, the finesse of the glass or crystal makes a difference too, particularly to the mouthfeel of a drink.

WHEN TO SERVE NEAT?

According to Adam Ford in his book *Vermouth*, the decline in vermouth consumption in the United States post World War II was due to the demand for 'stiffer' drinks and a shift away from drinking vermouth neat towards drinking it in cocktails, for which less and less vermouth was used, making way for stronger spirits.

Dry styles of vermouth are ideal for use as aperitifs as they often contain less sugar. Castagna Classic dry and Belsazar dry are two good examples, and both are ideal for sipping neat.

Vermouth really begins to come alive when served with simple accompaniments, as it is during Italian aperitivo. Mark Reginato, wine distributor extraordinaire, believes serving food with neat vermouth really enhances its texture: 'Maidenii unfiltered La Tonique (a quinquina) combined with silky anchovies, a pop of salty capers and crunchy croutons, really allows the dry, herbal and bitter notes of the vermouth to sing out.'

For entrée ...

The husband and wife team behind Banksii, Australia's first vermouth bar, are also strong advocates of serving neat vermouth with food and have created a delicious mussel entrée designed to complement a dry style of vermouth.

BANKSII'S MUSSELS IN VERMOUTH WITH GREEN OLIVES & NETTLE BUTTER

250 g (9 oz) cherry tomatoes

1 tablespoon olive oil, plus extra for drizzling

100 g (3½ oz) shallots, finely diced

1 kg (2 lb 3 oz) fresh mussels, scrubbed and debearded

150 ml (5 fl oz) Maidenii dry vermouth

150 g (5½ oz) green olives, pitted

picked watercress

sea salt and freshly ground black pepper

NETTLE BUTTER

30 ml (1 fl oz) olive oil

200 g (7 oz) fresh nettles, roughly chopped

200 g (7 oz) butter

To make the nettle butter, heat the olive oil in a frying pan over medium–high heat and sauté the nettles for 2–3 minutes, until just wilted. Transfer the nettles to a plate and refrigerate until completely cool.

Combine the butter and cooled nettles in a food processor and pulse to combine. Refrigerate the butter until ready to use.

Preheat the oven to 200°C (400°F).

Place the cherry tomatoes on a baking tray and drizzle over some olive oil. Season with salt and pepper, then roast in the oven for 10 minutes, or until the tomato skins have blistered. Set aside.

Heat the olive oil in a heavy-based saucepan over medium heat and sauté the shallots for 1 minute. Add the mussels and vermouth, cover with a lid, and simmer for 2–3 minutes, or until the mussels have opened. Discard any mussels that remain closed after cooking. Remove the cooked mussels and set aside.

Bring the cooking liquid to the boil and add the olives, then, working one spoonful at a time, gradually whisk in the nettle butter until it has all been incorporated. Add the cherry tomatoes and return the mussels to the saucepan. Stir briefly to coat, then transfer to a serving dish and garnish immediately with watercress.

VERMOUTH PAIRINGS *Rebecca suggests Ravensworth Outlandish Claims bitter tonic, Caperitif or Noilly Pratt dry vermouth to go with this dish.*

For dinner ...

The highly-talented Andreas Papadakis from the very successful restaurant Tipo 00 in Melbourne, suggests using vermouth to prepare his summer dish of trout, vermouth and orange.

TIPO 00'S CURED RAINBOW TROUT, VERMOUTH & BLOOD ORANGE

4 rainbow trout fillets, skinned and pin-boned, about 500 g (1 lb 2 oz)

poppy seeds and rocket (arugula) flowers, to garnish

CURE

25 g (1 oz) sea salt

2 blood oranges, zested and flesh cut into segments

30 ml (1 fl oz) vermouth

DRESSING

250 ml (8½ fl oz) fresh blood orange juice

75 ml (2½ fl oz) vegetable oil

25 ml (¾ fl oz) olive oil

15 ml (½ fl oz) vermouth

For the cure, mix together the sea salt, orange zest and vermouth in a bowl. Season the trout fillets all over with the curing mixture and leave to cure in the refrigerator for a minimum of 30 minutes and up to 2 hours (the longer the better). Wash off the cure and pat the fillets dry with paper towel.

To make the dressing, simmer the blood orange juice in a small saucepan over medium–high heat until the juice has reduced to 60 ml (2 fl oz). Transfer to a small bowl and leave to cool. Whisk in the oils, then whisk in the vermouth and set aside.

To serve, slice each trout fillet into 5 mm (¼ in) thick slices and arrange on four plates. Dress the fish generously with the dressing and garnish with fresh orange segments, a sprinkle of poppy seeds and rocket flowers.

TIP *For the best results, leave the fish to cure in the refrigerator for at least 2 hours before serving to allow the cure work through.*

Raul Moreno Yague, sommelier at Tipo 00, suggests Lustau vermut rojo from Jerez de la Frontera to accompany this dish:

'I have several reasons for choosing Lustau. First, its characteristics are quintessential of Spanish vermouth, which is traditionally sweeter than other styles. Lustau is also a great example of vermouth's sherry roots, with a nutty, salty edge and prunes that speak to Amontillado and Pedro Ximénez. Furthermore, the recipe includes only ten botanicals, including orange peel, wormwood, sage and coriander, all of which can be very easily detected. I find the moreishness of this particular vermouth fascinating, first appearing flabby and sweet, but once the mild bitterness builds up on your palate, the botanicals display themselves and take all your attention. This is a velvety, complex classic example of Spanish red vermouth to be drunk neat and sipped slowly.

For me, as a Spaniard, vermouth is a drink that denotes a time, a place and group of friends. The time varies from southern to northern Spain, but is usually between 1 and 1.30 pm. Traditionally, a group of close friends and/ or family will meet up to have a couple of glasses of vermouth before lunch to stimulate the appetite.'

Served with a meal, neat vermouth works best alongside strong, aromatic dishes that complement its botanical profile. Kylie Kwong, from the fantastic Sydney restaurant Billy Kwong, has provided us with her recipe for Crispy-skin duck with citrus sauce, matched with different vermouths selected by Billy Kwong wine buyer, Sophie Otton.

KYLIE KWONG'S CRISPY-SKIN DUCK WITH CITRUS SAUCE

1 × 1.5 kg (3 lb 5 oz) **free-range duck**

2 tablespoons **Sichuan pepper salt**

35 g (1¼ oz) **plain** (all-purpose) **flour**

safflower or sunflower oil, for deep-frying

CITRUS SAUCE

220 g (8 oz) **brown sugar**

80 ml (2½ fl oz) **fish sauce**

6 **star anise**

2 **cinnamon sticks**

juice of 3 limes

1 **orange**, peeled and sliced crossways

Rinse the duck under cold running water. Trim away any excess fat from inside and outside the cavity, and trim off the neck, parson's nose and winglets. Pat dry with paper towel and rub the skin all over with Sichuan pepper salt. Cover and leave to marinate in the refrigerator overnight.

Transfer the duck to a large steamer basket. Place the basket over a deep saucepan of boiling water and steam, covered securely, for approximately 1¼ hours, or until the duck is cooked through (to test, insert a small knife between the leg and the breast – the juices should run clear). Using tongs, gently remove the duck from the steamer and place it on a baking tray, breast-side up, to drain. Allow to cool slightly, then transfer to the refrigerator to cool further.

Meanwhile, make the citrus sauce. Combine the sugar with 250 ml (8½ fl oz) water in a small saucepan and bring to the boil. Reduce the heat to low and simmer, stirring occasionally, for about 7 minutes until slightly reduced.

Add the fish sauce and spices and simmer for another minute. Stir in the lime juice and orange, then remove the pan from the heat.

Place the cooled duck, breast-side up, on a chopping board and, using a large knife or meat cleaver, cut the duck in half lengthways through the breastbone and backbone. Carefully ease the meat away from the carcass, leaving the thighs, legs and wings intact. Because the duck has been cooked through completely, the meat should come away from the bones very easily. Lightly toss the duck halves in flour to coat, shaking off any excess.

Heat the oil in a hot wok until the surface seems to shimmer slightly. Deep-fry the duck halves, one at a time, for about 3 minutes each, turning once, or until well-browned and crispy. Using tongs, carefully remove the duck from the oil and drain well on paper towel, then leave to rest in a warm place for 5 minutes while you gently reheat the citrus sauce.

Finally, use a sharp knife to cut the duck into pieces, then arrange on a serving platter. Spoon over the hot citrus sauce and serve immediately.

VERMOUTH PAIRINGS *Sophie suggests Maidenii 19 Botanicals, Golfo tinto old vine, Regal Rogue Bold red.*

For a cheese course ...

Vermouth is an interesting candidate. In Anglo-Saxon culture, the pairing of cheese and fortified wine is traditional, with Port and Stilton or Amontillado and Manchego viejo. Here, Nicola Munari, managing director of London's Taillevent wine bar and bottle shop, reveals his Piemontese roots by using vermouth instead of Port to balance the salty taste of Stilton:

'Pairing Stilton with Port or sloe gin would be easy, safe and efficient. Pairing it with Italian vermouth might seem more ambitious but, in reality, allows you to get the best out of both ingredients.

The result is a whole new taste experience, combining caressing sweetness, juicy fruitiness, an irresistible spicy twist and balsamic lift, all there to enrobe and embellish the flavours of creamy and mouldy Stilton. It revitalises the tastebuds, opening the palate up to an array of options for a digestif or a cocktail to end the meal.'

VERMOUTH PAIRINGS *Nicola suggests Maidenii sweet, Mancino rosso amaranto, Cocchi Storico di Torino.*

For dessert ...

Vermouth is at its most celebrated when matched with a dessert. Depending on its dominant flavour, be it caramel, vanilla, fruit or mint, sweet vermouth can be served with a vast range of desserts. Here, the crème de la crème of Australian chefs, Ben Shewry of Attica in Melbourne, shows just how versatile vermouth can be.

BEN SHEWRY'S PEAR & VERMOUTH DESSERT

fresh rosemary flowers, to garnish

MAIDENII SORBET

4 litres (135 fl oz) **fresh cow's milk**

3 g (⅛ oz) **powdered rennet**

300 g (10½ oz) **sugar**

200 g (7 oz) **trimoline**

500 g (1 lb 2 oz) **sheep's milk yoghurt**

Maidenii Classic vermouth, for seasoning

First, we start by making a fresh soft cheese. To do this, we heat the cow's milk to 30°C (86°F) then add the powdered rennet. We allow the milk to sit at room temperature for 12 hours, then suspend it in a piece of muslin (cheesecloth), over a container to capture the whey, in the refrigerator for another 12 hours to firm up. Reserve 200 g (7 oz) of the cheese whey. This recipe yields 500 g (1 lb 2 oz) cow's milk cheese.

Once we have the cheese, we can make the sorbet. To do this, we combine the cheese whey (from hanging the cheese), the sugar and trimoline in a saucepan and heat until the sugar has dissolved. In a bowl, we whisk the fresh cheese and sheep's milk yoghurt together until smooth then add the sugar mixture. Once this mixture is well combined, we season the sorbet with the vermouth – add as much or as little as you like. Pour into Paco canisters and freeze until ready to serve.

FRUIT-SPICED PEAR BALLS

beurre bosc pear

750 g (1 lb 11 oz) **caster** (superfine) **sugar**

80 g (2¾ oz) **fruit spice**

35 g (1¼ oz) **citric acid**

g (⅛ oz) **fine sea salt**

Preheat the oven to 220°C (430°F). Peel the pear, then, using a very small melon baller, scoop out 12 balls of pear.

We combine the sugar, fruit spice, citric acid and salt, then dust the pear balls in the spiced sugar and roast on a baking tray in the oven at for 1–2 minutes, or until they begin to caramelise.

DEHYDRATED PEAR SKINS

690 g (1½ lb) **caster** (superfine) **sugar**

250 ml (8½ fl oz) **sweet-apple vinegar, boiled and chilled skin of 1 pear, peeled with a vegetable peeler**

Combine the sugar, 500 ml (17 fl oz) water and sweet-apple vinegar and compress the pear skin in the mixture. Remove the skins from the syrup and lay them on a baking tray to dehydrate overnight. The skins should become crunchy and crinkled.

PEAR VINEGAR

950 g (2 lb 2 oz) **brown pears, peeled and grated**

830 g (1 lb 13 oz) **sweet-apple vinegar**

200 g (7 oz) **caster** (superfine) **sugar**

To make the pear vinegar, we combine the grated pear with the vinegar and compress in a bag. We then cook the pear in a water bath at 50°C (122°F) for 1 hour. It is then transferred to the refrigerator and left to infuse overnight. The cold liquid is passed through a piece of muslin (cheesecloth) before the sugar is added. The vinegar and sure are then heated gently on the stove until the sugar has dissolved and the mixture has reduced slightly.

We garnish the dessert with a few drops of pear vinegar and some rosemary flowers.

VERMOUTH PAIRINGS *Jane Lopes suggests Mauro Vergano, Otto's Athens and Margot's Off-sweet.*

INDRA CARRILLO'S VERMOUTH & WATERMELON DESSERT

Indra Carrillo, and his first restaurant La Condesa, is one to watch in Paris, with his fulsome CV and a cuisine of multiple influences. He also uses vermouth in his dessert of Watermelon, hibiscus sorbet, pomegranate and candied tomato with vermouth jelly and smoked mezcal salt.

VERMOUTH PAIRINGS *Alexandre Jean suggests Maidenii Classic and La Quintinye rouge.*

NEAT VERMOUTH AROUND THE WORLD

The champion drinkers of neat vermouth are, without doubt, the Spanish. You can visit almost any bar and they will have a *vermut della casa*, or 'house vermouth', served simply from a bottle or on tap, next to the beer. The vermouth on tap, called *vermut de grifo*, is usually quite cheap and served in a tumbler. Their bottled vermouths are often sweet, dark, and use a limited number of botanicals. The Italians also serve vermouth during their ritual aperitivo, where they drink it over ice garnished with a citrus twist.

In this, the contemporary era, the new wave of vermouths are usually consumed neat, served mostly in bars and the best restaurants.

One of my favourite ways to serve neat vermouth is as a digestif, enjoyed with a fine cigar on a warm summer evening. An amaro or a medium-dry style of vermouth is ideal for this.

HANDLING OF VERMOUTH

Being fortified, vermouth will remain more stable than wine, particularly when stored in the fridge. Once opened, vermouth will not change radically, but will gradually lose its freshness and intensity. If you only plan to drink vermouth sporadically, buying a half-bottle is a good alternative, as it won't have to be stored as long. Rest assured, using chilled vermouth in cocktails won't have an adverse effect on their flavour or the intensity of their aromatics.

As vermouth is a wine, you could cellar it. Often the closures on vermouths are screw caps and this can be an advantage when ageing vermouths, as screw caps ensure slower evolution compared to corks. It is best to store screw capped bottles horizontally as this allows you to check the quality of the seal. With cellaring, there is a second market for old vermouths or bitters at auction.

Vermouth is not as expensive as some wines, but one of the most expensive cocktails on record contained vermouth and was created by Salvatore Calabrese at The Playboy Club in London in a Guinness World Record attempt in October 2012. Its astronomical price tag of AUD$6,700 was due to its combination of decadent vintage ingredients, including a 1778 Clos de Griffier Vieux cognac, a 1770 Kummel liqueur, an 1860 Dubb Orange Curaçao and a tiny bottle of nineteenth-century Angostura bitters. This is also believed to be the oldest cocktail in the world, with the ingredients having a combined age of 730 years.

SPRING

Spring is an exciting season, and the first sign of sun after a long winter is always something to celebrate.

Cherries begin to appear and are at their best late in the season. Strawberries start popping up in markets and, my favourite, the humble pea makes its way into my drinks. Spring cocktails are all about light flavours and freshness, plus a few robust drinks for the still-cool evenings.

In spring, the vermouthery is a hive of activity as we collect and macerate fresh botanicals as well as some dried ones towards the end of the season. This is also the time of year we plan how much we want to produce for the following year, and we start visiting the vineyards in central Victoria to check their health and plan the vintage with the growers.

NASTURTIUM FRAPPÉ

(pictured opposite)

The inspiration for this cocktail came from the Absinthe Frappé, a New Orleans classic made of absinthe, mint, sugar and, in some cases, soda water (club soda). Absentroux also produce absinthe, so it's no surprise that this is an incredibly wormwood-driven vermouth.

45 ml (1½ fl oz) **Absentroux vermouth**
15 ml (½ fl oz) **Nasturtium Leaf Absinthe** (see below)
8 mint leaves
ice cubes, for shaking
crushed ice, to serve
fresh nasturtium flowers and a mint sprig, to garnish

NASTURTIUM LEAF ABSINTHE (MAKES 200 ML/7 FL OZ)

20 g (¾ oz) **fresh nasturtium leaves**
200 ml (7 fl oz) **absinthe**

To make the nasturtium leaf absinthe, prepare a bowl of iced water and set aside. Bring a small saucepan of water to the boil and blanch the leaves for 30 seconds. Drain, and immediately transfer the leaves to the iced water.

Drain the leaves, place in a pestle and mortar and grind to a paste. Add the absinthe and leave to macerate for 2 hours. Strain the absinthe through a piece of muslin (cheesecloth) into a jug, discarding the leaves. Pour into a sterilised glass bottle (see page 78) and seal tightly. Store in the refrigerator for up to 2 months.

To make a Nasturtium Frappé, add all the ingredients to a cocktail shaker and top with ice cubes. Shake vigorously for 10 seconds, then strain into a chilled absinthe glass filled with crushed ice. Garnish with nasturtium flowers and a mint sprig.

PINK PEACH

Quandongs, also known as native peaches, are indigenous to Australia. While it can be difficult to find fresh ones, dried quandongs are readily available in Australia from outbackchef.com.au and are perfect for making the bitter-tasting syrup in this cocktail. The juicy berry characters of this rosé vermouth pair well with the quandongs.

60 ml (2 fl oz) **Adelaide Hills Distillery rosé vermouth**
30 ml (1 fl oz) **Quandong Syrup** (see below)
90 ml (3 fl oz) **ginger beer**
ice cubes, to serve
lime wedge and Candied Quandongs (see below), **to garnish**

QUANDONG SYRUP & CANDIED QUANDONGS
(MAKES APPROX. 350 ML/12 FL OZ)

50 g (1¾ oz) **dried quandongs**
300 g (10½ oz) **caster** (superfine) **sugar**
25 ml (¾ fl oz) **apple-cider vinegar**

Prepare the quandongs and syrup by combining all the ingredients in a saucepan with 300 ml (10 fl oz) water. Bring to the boil, then reduce the heat and simmer for 30 minutes. Strain through a fine-mesh sieve into a jug and set the rehydrated quandongs aside. Pour the syrup into a sterilised glass bottle (see page 78) and seal tightly. Store in the refrigerator for up to 1 week.

Transfer the quandongs to a food dehydrator and leave to dry out for 2 hours. Alternatively, spread the quandongs on a baking tray and dry out for 2 hours in an oven preheated to the lowest possible setting.

For the Pink Peach, add the vermouth and syrup to a chilled Collins glass and gently pour in the ginger beer. Carefully top with ice cubes, then garnish with a lime wedge and candied quandongs.

GROWING UP
IN THE FOREST

(pictured opposite)

I grew up on rhubarb. My mum
would stew it and serve it
with ice cream, and the smell
of it cooking takes me back
to that time. My first taste of
sarsaparilla was on a camping
trip in the woods when I was
younger. These two flavours
combine quite well and Ransom
sweet vermouth always reminds
me of both sarsaparilla and my
mum's stewed rhubarb.

60 ml (2 fl oz) **Ransom sweet vermouth**

60 ml (2 fl oz) **sarsaparilla**

ice cubes, to serve

50 ml (1¾ fl oz) **Rhubarb Foam** (see below)**, to garnish**

RHUBARB FOAM (MAKES APPROX. 400 ML/13½ FL OZ)

200 g (7 oz) **rhubarb stalks, roughly chopped**

350 g (12½ oz) **caster** (superfine) **sugar**

2 cm (¾ in) **piece of vanilla bean, seeds scraped**

10 g (¼ oz) **citric acid**

2 **egg whites**

To make the rhubarb foam, combine the rhubarb, sugar and vanilla bean and
seeds in a saucepan with 650 ml (22 fl oz) water. Bring to the boil, then reduce
the heat to medium and simmer for 30 minutes.

Strain the liquid through a fine-mesh sieve into a bowl, add the citric acid
and stir to dissolve. Set aside to cool completely. Once cool, combine 800 ml
(27 fl oz) of the rhubarb syrup with the egg whites in a cream siphon and
double-charge. If you don't have a siphon, simply whisk the syrup with the egg
whites until light, aerated, and strong enough to float on top of the drink.

For the cocktail, add the vermouth to a chilled rocks glass, then gently pour in
the sarsaparilla. Carefully top with ice to retain the fizz. Float the rhubarb foam
on top to serve.

PEA MARTINI

Nothing says spring more than
fresh garden peas. Though a bit
of an uncommon combination,
the peas give the gin an
extra aromatic boost. For the
vermouth, something a little
sweeter but not too sweet,
like Martini Riserva Speciale
Ambrato, gives the drink floral
honey notes that pair well with
the aromatics in the pea gin.

45 ml (1½ fl oz) **Martini Riserva Speciale Ambrato vermouth**

45 ml (1½ fl oz) **Pea Gin** (see below)

dash of Saline Solution (page 77)

ice cubes, for mixing

mint leaf, to garnish

PEA GIN (MAKES 300 ML/10 FL OZ)

10 g (¼ oz) **snow pea** (mange tout) **tendrils**

50 g (1¾ oz) **fresh peas, podded**

300 ml (10 fl oz) **Bombay Sapphire gin**

Prepare the pea gin by combining all the ingredients in a bowl. Cover and
leave to macerate for 12 hours or overnight. Strain the gin through a fine-mesh
sieve into a sterilised glass bottle (see page 78) and seal tightly. Store in the
refrigerator for up to 1 month.

To make a Pea Martini, add all the ingredients to a mixing glass and top with
ice cubes. Stir, to chill and dilute, for about 20 seconds.

Strain into a chilled Coupette glass and garnish with a mint leaf.

SWEET TEA SODA

This cocktail was developed for a friend of mine, John Parker, when he opened his bar, Halford, in Perth. It's a long drink made with tea and vermouth and freshened with dry cider and a strawberry purée float that gives the drink a lovely nose every time you take a sip.

45 ml (1½ fl oz) **Maidenii sweet vermouth**
60 ml (2 fl oz) **Black Tea Syrup** (see below)
90 ml (3 fl oz) **dry apple cider**
ice cubes, to serve
50 ml (1¾ fl oz) **strawberry purée, to serve**
a mint sprig, to garnish

BLACK TEA SYRUP (MAKES 350 ML/12 FL OZ)

20 g (¾ oz) **Darjeeling black tea leaves**
100 g (3½ oz) **caster** (superfine) **sugar**

Make the black tea syrup by combining the tea leaves with 400 ml (13½ fl oz) chilled, filtered water in a large bowl. Leave to macerate for 1 hour, stirring every 10 minutes.

Strain the liquid through a fine-mesh sieve, discarding the tea. Return the liquid to the bowl and add the sugar, stirring vigorously to dissolve. Pour the syrup into a sterilised glass bottle (see page 78) and seal tightly. Store in the refrigerator for up to 1 week.

To make a Sweet Tea Soda, combine the vermouth and tea syrup in a chilled Collins glass. Gently pour in the cider and carefully top with ice cubes to retain the fizz. Float the strawberry purée on top, then garnish with a mint sprig.

SCANDINAVIAN FROST

The older I get, the more I like fennel. I like everything about the plant: the vegetable, the fragrant seeds and the aromatic profile of the pollen. Here, I have matched it with aquavit, a traditional Scandinavian spirit aromatised with a mixture of spices, including caraway. Dolin vermouths are on the lighter side, which makes their dry version perfect for this cocktail.

50 ml (1¾ fl oz) **Dolin dry vermouth**

10 ml (¼ fl oz) **aquavit**

10 ml (¼ fl oz) **Fennel Pollen Syrup** (see below)

dash of orange bitters

rock ice, to serve

fennel fronds and a lemon twist, to garnish

FENNEL POLLEN SYRUP (MAKES APPROX. 600 ML/20½ FL OZ)

500 g (1 lb 2 oz) **caster** (superfine) **sugar**

10 g (¼ oz) **fennel pollen**

First, make the fennel pollen syrup. Combine the sugar and pollen in a saucepan with 500 ml (17 fl oz) water and bring to the boil. Reduce the heat to medium and simmer for 30 minutes.

Strain the syrup through a piece of muslin (cheesecloth) into a jug, discarding the pollen. Pour into a sterilised glass bottle (see page 78) and seal tightly. Store in the refrigerator for up to 1 week.

For a Scandinavian Forest, mix together all the ingredients except the ice in a chilled Old Fashioned glass and stir with a bar spoon. Add a block of rock ice, stir to chill and dilute, then garnish with fennel fronds and a lemon twist.

CHERRY BOLD SOUR

Mark Ward, who owns Australian vermouth company Regal Rogue, must be credited with the creation of this cocktail. His Bold red vermouth is not as sweet as other red vermouths; in fact it only has 80 g (2¾ oz) of sugar, putting it in the semi-dry category. Essentially a vermouth sour, I have taken Mark's recipe and added some cherry juice.

60 ml (2 fl oz) **Regal Rogue Bold red vermouth**

30 ml (1 fl oz) **lemon juice**

10 ml (¼ fl oz) **egg white**

5 ml (⅛ fl oz) **Marasca cherry soaking juice, from the jar**

ice cubes, for shaking

orange twist and Marasca cherries, to garnish

Combine all the ingredients in a cocktail shaker and top with ice cubes. Shake vigorously for 10 seconds, then strain into a small chilled wine glass and garnish with an orange twist and some Marasca cherries.

CYN CYN

This cocktail comes from a friend of mine, Camille Ralph Vidal, who is the global brand ambassador for St Germain, a wonderful elderflower liqueur. Noilly Prat extra dry is the vermouth of choice here, as it has delicate floral notes and a slightly salty finish that harmonises perfectly with the other ingredients.

20 ml (¾ fl oz) **Noilly Prat extra dry vermouth**
20 ml (¾ fl oz) **Bombay Sapphire gin**
10 ml (¼ fl oz) **St Germain**
10 ml (¼ fl oz) **Cynar**
ice cubes, for mixing
orange twist, to garnish

Combine all the ingredients in a mixing glass and top with ice cubes. Stir, to chill and dilute, for about 20 seconds.

Strain into a chilled Coupette glass and garnish with an orange twist.

ARMY, NAVY & THE MARINES

The classic Army & Navy cocktail combines gin, lemon juice and orgeat, an almond-flavoured syrup. I thought it would be great to change up the classic by adding vermouth and a dose of salt. The West Winds actually use salt in their gin production, so it works rather well. For the vermouth, I have used Mancino secco, which is fairly dry and flavoured with Mediterranean herbs that are prominent on the palate.

20 ml (¾ fl oz) **Mancino secco vermouth**
20 ml (¾ fl oz) **The West Winds Broadside gin**
20 ml (¾ fl oz) **orgeat**
20 ml (¾ fl oz) **lemon juice**
dash of Saline Solution (page 77)
ice cubes, for shaking
coconut flakes, to garnish

Combine all the ingredients in a cocktail shaker and top with ice cubes. Shake vigorously for 10 seconds, then strain into a chilled cocktail glass and garnish with coconut flakes.

MELBOURNE FRUIT CUP

(pictured opposite)

What is Spring without a fruit cup? Classically made with Pimms – a gin-based aperitif sweetened and flavoured with herbs – fruit cups, also known as summer cups, can be made simply with gin and vermouth, like this version. You can use whatever brands you like, but I have opted exclusively for products that have been produced in Melbourne, to make this a truly Melbournian fruit cup.

30 ml (1 fl oz) **Maidenii Classic vermouth**
30 ml (1 fl oz) **Melbourne Gin Company gin**
45 ml (1½ fl oz) **Capi dry ginger ale**
45 ml (1½ fl oz) **Capi lemonade**
ice cubes
strawberry fan and a basil leaf, to garnish

Combine the vermouth and gin in a chilled Collins glass, then gently pour in the ginger ale and lemonade.

Carefully top with ice cubes to retain the fizz, then garnish with a strawberry fan and a basil leaf.

CHERRY JULEP

The classic cocktail Mint Julep is synonymous with racing. In particular, the Kentucky Derby in the United States. Cherry and bourbon go so well together, but they are big flavours and need a big vermouth to match. Enter Carpano Antica Formula, a very rich, textural, sweet vermouth that works incredibly well with the strong-flavoured spirits of the world.

45 ml (1½ fl oz) **Carpano Antica Formula vermouth**
45 ml (1½ fl oz) **Cherry Bourbon** (see below)
8 mint leaves
crushed ice
a mint sprig and icing (confectioners') **sugar, to garnish**
CHERRY BOURBON (MAKES APPROX. 750 ML/25½ FL OZ)

200 g (7 oz) **fresh cherries, pitted**
700 ml (23½ fl oz) **bourbon**

To make the cherry bourbon, muddle the cherries in a bowl then pour in the bourbon. Cover, and leave to macerate for 24 hours. Strain the bourbon through a fine-mesh sieve into a sterilised glass bottle (see page 78) and seal tightly. Mix the smashed cherries with the same weight of 2:1 Sugar Syrup (page 77) and store in the freezer, ready to use as a topping for ice cream.

Make a Cherry Julep by combining all the ingredients except the ice in a chilled julep cup. Top with crushed ice and mix vigorously with a bar spoon. Top with more crushed ice and garnish with a mint sprig and a sprinkling of icing sugar.

Corpse Revivers are a family of classic cocktails that use both vermouth and quinquina, an aromatised wine made with cinchona bark.

These recipes are from Sebastian Raeburn – distiller, industry advocate and cocktail enthusiast.

CORPSE REVIVER #1

A simple blend of brandy, Calvados (apple brandy) and sweet vermouth. The ideal time to drink this would be after a large meal sitting next to an open fire on a cool spring evening.

20 ml (¾ fl oz) Maidenii sweet vermouth
30 ml (1 fl oz) brandy
10 ml (¼ fl oz) Calvados
ice cubes, for mixing
orange twist, to garnish

Combine all the ingredients in a mixing glass and top with ice cubes. Stir to chill and dilute for about 20 seconds.

Strain into a chilled Nick & Nora glass and garnish with an orange twist.

CORPSE REVIVER #2

This cocktail first appeared in the 1930 edition of Harry Craddock's *Savoy Cocktail Book*. It's one of those drinks that just works; the flavours are at once clearly defined and beautifully mixed. A truly classic drink and, as Harry Craddock said, '... four of these, taken in succession, will revive the corpse again'. Those were the days!

20 ml (¾ fl oz) Maidenii quinquina
30 ml (1 fl oz) Anther gin
20 ml (¾ fl oz) lemon juice
20 ml (¾ fl oz) orange liqueur
5 ml (⅛ fl oz) absinthe
ice cubes, for shaking
orange twist, to garnish

Combine all the ingredients in a cocktail shaker and top with ice cubes. Shake vigorously for 10 seconds, then strain into a chilled cocktail glass and garnish with an orange twist.

CORPSE REVIVER #BLUE

Jacob Briars created this drink and brought it to international fame at a series of seminars we did together at Tales of the Cocktail in 2009. Jacob has been known to walk into very serious establishments and ask for a Corpse Reviver Number Blue. Quite often the formal bars do not stock the infamous Blue Curaçao required. Never fear, Jacob is the only cocktail aficionado who can sometimes be spotted sporting a hip flask of Blue Curaçao for just these occasions.

20 ml (¾ fl oz) Maidenii quinquina
30 ml (1 fl oz) Anther gin
20 ml (¾ fl oz) lemon juice
20 ml (¾ fl oz) Blue Curaçao
5 ml (⅛ fl oz) absinthe
ice cubes, for shaking
orange twist, to garnish

Combine all the ingredients in a cocktail shaker and top with ice cubes. Shake vigorously for 10 seconds, then strain into a chilled cocktail glass and garnish with an orange twist.

SUMMER

The hottest season of the year calls for tropical and stone fruits for your cocktails.

With the heat often comes dehydration, so I prefer to drink beverages with a lower alcohol content. Cocktails in summer should be fun, frivolous, minimal fuss and, most importantly, refreshing.

Summer is a busy time in the vermouthery. We are finishing off the tinctures, or botanical macerates, by filtering and blending them into master tinctures ready for fortifying the wine. We are also checking the vineyards frequently as we approach vintage time. The end of summer heralds the beginning of vintage and we get to work picking, pressing and fermenting.

BLUEBERRY SPRITZ

(pictured opposite)

My favourite part of this drink is the blueberry verjus. It's such a simple thing to make and has so many uses. It's lovely added to a gin and tonic, and it's delightful in place of vinegar in a salad dressing. The vermouth we have used here is made in the Yarra Valley in Victoria. It's quite dry by vermouth standards and has delightful hints of quinine bitterness and citrus notes.

60 ml (2 fl oz) **Causes & Cures semi-dry white vermouth**
60 ml (2 fl oz) **Blueberry Verjus** (see below)
5 ml (⅛ fl oz) **Canadian maple syrup**
30 ml (1 fl oz) **prosecco**
ice cubes, to serve
fresh blueberries and a lemon twist, to garnish

BLUEBERRY VERJUS (MAKES APPROX. 450–500 ML/15–17 FL OZ)

250 g (9 oz) **blueberries**
500 ml (17 fl oz) **verjus**

First, make the blueberry verjus. Start a day ahead and freeze your blueberries overnight. Combine the frozen blueberries with the verjus in a bowl and leave to macerate for 12 hours.

Strain the verjus through a fine-mesh sieve into a sterilised glass bottle (see page 78), discarding the blueberries. Seal tightly and store in the refrigerator for 1–2 weeks.

To make a Blueberry Spritz, combine the vermouth, verjus and maple syrup in a chilled Burgundy glass and stir gently to combine. Carefully pour in the prosecco and top with ice cubes to retain the fizz. Serve garnished with fresh blueberries and a lemon twist.

PEACH ICED TEA

I've always liked using tea in cocktails; there is a huge variety of flavour despite all teas coming from the same plant, *Camellia sinensis*. Here, I've used a black tea for the syrup. Chilling the maceration removes many of the tannins and gives the tea a lighter flavour that works well with the peach. I have chosen Casa Mariol *vermut* for this cocktail as Casa Mariol use over 130 botanicals in their vermouths, making them more savoury and a perfect partner to fruits.

¾ of a fresh whole peach, stoned and roughly chopped
60 ml (2 fl oz) **Casa Mariol vermut blanco**
15 ml (½ fl oz) **Black Tea Syrup** (see below)
10 ml (¼ fl oz) **lemon juice**
ice cubes, for shaking
crushed ice, to serve
peach wedge and a mint sprig, to garnish

BLACK TEA SYRUP (MAKES APPROX. 500 ML/17 FL OZ)

40 g (1½ oz) **Darjeeling black tea leaves**
200 g (7 oz) **caster** (superfine) **sugar**

For the black tea syrup, put the tea leaves in a large bowl and pour in 400 ml (13½ fl oz) chilled, filtered water. Leave to macerate for 1 hour, stirring every 10 minutes.

Strain the syrup through a fine-mesh sieve and return to the bowl. Add the sugar and stir vigorously until the sugar has dissolved. Pour into a sterilised glass bottle (see page 78) and seal tightly. Store in the refrigerator for 1 week.

To make a Peach Iced Tea, muddle the peach in a cocktail shaker until crushed to a pulp. Add the remaining ingredients and top with ice cubes. Shake vigorously for 10 seconds, then strain into a chilled julep cup over crushed ice. Garnish with a peach wedge and a mint sprig to serve.

EL APRICOTO

(pictured opposite)

Traditionally a sherry producer, Lustau also make vermouth, and this one combines mostly amontillado and a little Pedro Ximénez as the base wine. Certainly on the sweeter side, this cocktail needs a dash of salt and some fresh citrus to help balance the sugar. Take it to the next level by serving it with some smoked almonds. I don't know why, but it just works.

45 ml (1½ fl oz) **Lustau rojo vermut**
15 ml (½ fl oz) **apricot brandy liqueur**
30 ml (1 fl oz) **red grapefruit juice**
10 ml (¼ fl oz) **manzanilla sherry**
4 drops **InstaFoam** (page 85)
dash of **Saline Solution** (page 77)
½ **apricot**
ice cubes, for shaking
red grapefruit twist, to garnish
smoked almonds, to serve

Combine all the ingredients except the ice in a cocktail shaker and shake vigorously for 10 seconds. Open the shaker and top with ice cubes, then seal and shake for another 10 seconds.

Strain into a chilled Coupette glass and garnish with a grapefruit twist. Serve a small bowl of smoked almonds on the side.

TIP *If you're in Australia, you can purchase InstaFoam at onlybitters.com.au.*

BLACKBERRY TONIC

Causes & Cures semi sweet vermouth is made with biodynamic Sangiovese grapes from the Yarra Valley in Victoria. The wine component in this vermouth is certainly in the driver's seat, with the botanicals in the back. A simple blend of this with some tonic and a little crème de mûre make an excellent summer highball. One note on the crème de mûre: whatever brand you get, make sure you keep it in the fridge; lower-alcohol berry liqueurs tend to oxidise and change flavour if left for too long at room temperature.

50 ml (1¾ fl oz) **Causes & Cures semi sweet red vermouth**
10 ml (¼ fl oz) **crème de mûre**
100 ml (3½ fl oz) **tonic water**
ice cubes, to serve
fresh blackberries and a lemon wedge, to garnish

Add the vermouth and crème de mûre to a chilled highball glass and pour in the tonic. Gently top with ice cubes to retain the fizz.

Garnish with fresh blackberries and a lemon wedge to serve.

VERMOUTH MARY

There is nothing better than a Bloody Mary in the morning, or is there? If we look at the humble tomato and what herbs work best with it, there are many similarities with the botanical DNA of vermouth. A lot of dry vermouths will work with this recipe, but my favourite is Maidenii dry vermouth (for obvious reasons). I find the native savoury elements really shine with the viscous tomato water.

ice cubes

60 ml (2 fl oz) Maidenii dry vermouth

100 ml (3½ fl oz) Spiced Tomato Water (see below)

a cucumber spear, pickled ginger and Tabasco sauce, to garnish

SPICED TOMATO WATER (MAKES 1.25 LITRES/42 FL OZ)

2 kg (4 lb 6 oz) beefsteak tomatoes, stems removed

10 fresh celery leaves

2 red bird's eye chillies, stems removed

10 g (¼ oz) sea salt flakes

20 ml (¾ fl oz) sherry vinegar

To make the spiced tomato water, combine all the ingredients in a food processor and blitz to a purée.

Line a fine-mesh sieve with a piece of muslin (cheesecloth) and suspend it over a large bowl. Pour in the tomato water and leave to drain for 2 hours. Pour the drained tomato water into a sterilised glass bottle (see page 78). Seal tightly and store for in the refrigerator for up to 1 week. Reserve the tomato pulp for making passata.

For a Vermouth Mary, fill a chilled highball glass with ice cubes. Pour in the vermouth and tomato water and give it a stir. Garnish with a cucumber spear, some pickled ginger and a few dashes of Tabasco sauce to serve.

MANGO BUCK

(pictured opposite)

For me, nothing screams summer more than the smell of a ripe mango. I have fond childhood memories of doing my best to get every last bit of sweet flesh off the skin, dribbling a lot of juice down my chin in the process. If you can get hold of them, Kensington Pride mangoes are among my favourite varieties, and they work incredibly well with the spicier notes of Maidenii dry vermouth.

60 ml (2 fl oz) **Mango Maidenii** (see below)
90 ml (3 fl oz) **ginger beer**
ice cubes, to serve
lime wedge and mango slice, to garnish

MANGO MAIDENII (MAKES 750 ML/25½ FL OZ)

1 fresh whole **mango**
750 ml (25½ fl oz) **Maidenii dry vermouth**

To make the Mango Maidenii, cut the skin and flesh off the mango and discard the pit. Combine the mango skin and flesh with the vermouth in a sealable bag (ideally vacuum sealed), and leave to macerate for 12 hours or overnight.

Strain the vermouth through a fine-mesh sieve into a sterilised glass bottle (see page 78) and seal tightly. Store in the refrigerator for up to 2 weeks.

For a Mango Buck, add the Mango Maidenii to a chilled highball glass and pour in the ginger beer. Top with ice cubes to retain the fizz, and garnish with a lime wedge and mango slice to serve.

INVERSE CLOVER CLUB

This cocktail comes from a friend of mine, Edward Quatermass – the man behind the bar at Maker in Brisbane. The classic Clover Club cocktail is an equally delicious drink, which calls for a larger serving of gin and a smaller serving of vermouth. Here, that ratio has been reversed. The gin here is from our friends at Four Pillars, who macerate Shiraz grapes into their gin to create Four Pillars Shiraz gin. Our dry vermouth is the perfect complement, as both drinks share many of the same botanicals.

40 ml (1¼ fl oz) **Maidenii dry vermouth**
20 ml (¾ fl oz) **Four Pillars Shiraz gin**
20 ml (¾ fl oz) **lemon juice**
10 ml (¼ fl oz) **2:1 Sugar Syrup** (page 77)
4 fresh **raspberries**
10 ml (¼ fl oz) **egg white**
dash of **Saline Solution** (page 77)
ice cubes, for shaking
fresh raspberries on a toothpick, to garnish

Combine all the ingredients except the ice in a cocktail shaker and shake vigorously for 10 seconds. Open the shaker and top with ice cubes, then seal and shake for another 10 seconds.

Strain into a chilled Coupette glass and garnish with a toothpick of raspberries.

POMPIER

 HUGH LEECH

The Pompier (meaning a firefighter in French), Highball or Vermouth Cassis, is France's answer to the Aperol Spritz. It is an elegant, all-French aperitif that combines refreshment with a beautiful pink hue. While the origin of the name seems lost, the cocktail first emerged in the popular Parisian-style cafes of New York in the 1930s following the repeal of Prohibition. The fantastic herbal complexity from the vermouth and the bright, rich fruit from the Cassis play together to create a true dark horse of the aperitif world.

45 ml (1½ fl oz) **Maidenii dry vermouth**
15 ml (½ fl oz) **Marionette Cassis**
60 ml (2 fl oz) **soda water** (club soda)
ice cubes, to serve
lemon wedge, to garnish

Combine the vermouth and Cassis in a chilled highball glass and top with the soda water.

Gently add ice cubes to retain the fizz and garnish with a lemon wedge.

BRONX

 SEBASTIAN RAEBURN

In the 1920s, around the time this cocktail rose to fame, oranges were not gas-ripened in cooled warehouses like they are today – they had the natural sugars, acids and vitamins necessary to make this cocktail sing. I have experimented with oranges ripened on the tree and picked fresh and they beat shop-bought oranges hands down.

15 ml (½ fl oz) **Dolin rouge vermouth**
15 ml (½ fl oz) **Dolin dry vermouth**
40 ml (1¼ fl oz) **Anther gin**
20 ml (¾ fl oz) **fresh orange juice**
ice cubes, for shaking
orange twist, to garnish

Combine all the ingredients in a cocktail shaker and top with ice cubes. Shake vigorously for 10 seconds, then strain into a chilled Coupette glass and garnish with an orange twist.

LITTLE BIT FANCY LYCHEE MARTINI

I've seen quite a lot of recipes for Lychee Martinis in my time, ranging from lychee vodka with vermouth, to mocktail versions using the juice from the can with fresh citrus. I'm a big fan of verjus and it works perfectly in this recipe to take the edge off the sweet lychee syrup. A note about tinned lychees: not all were created equal, so I would encourage you to sample a few and find a brand that you like. The Regal Rogue vermouth works well here as it is quite savoury, giving a nice contrast to the fruitiness of the cocktail.

30 ml (1 fl oz) **Regal Rogue Daring dry vermouth**
30 ml (1 fl oz) **vodka**
20 ml (¾ fl oz) **lychee syrup from tinned lychees**
10 ml (¼ fl oz) **verjus**
5 ml (⅛ fl oz) **2:1 Sugar Syrup** (page 77)
ice cubes, for mixing
lemon twist and lychees on a toothpick, to garnish

Combine all the ingredients in a mixing glass and top with ice cubes. Stir to chill and dilute for about 20 seconds.

Strain into a chilled cocktail glass and garnish with a lemon twist and toothpick of lychees.

AUTUMN (FALL)

Apples and pomegranates and quinces, oh my! These are just a few of my favourite flavours, as they are easily relatable to the season and offer a fresh foil to the warmer autumn days.

The more robust autumnal flavours also work well with spicier ingredients for those cooler evenings.

Vintage continues throughout autumn at the vermouthery, with fermenting, blending and maturation. It is also the time that we fortify the wines with their master tincture to turn them into vermouth. This is quite possibly the busiest time of year for us and Gilles doesn't like it if I take any holidays.

SLOE SPIDER

(pictured opposite)

Spiders were always a treat growing up. To a kid, they are the perfect combination of soft drink and ice cream.

As I got a little older, alcohol made its way into the spiders and, once I began producing vermouth, that made its way in too. Castagna's dry vermouth is great in this cocktail as the savoury elements balance out the sweetness. The matcha tea sprinkled on top is a must, as it really helps to bring all the elements together.

30 ml (1 fl oz) **Castagna Classic dry vermouth**
30 ml (1 fl oz) **Sipsmith sloe gin**
50 ml (1¾ fl oz) **apple cider**
50 ml (1¾ fl oz) **lemonade**
1 scoop vanilla ice cream, to serve
matcha powder, to garnish

Combine the vermouth and gin in a chilled Collins glass. Gently top with the cider and lemonade, then finish with a scoop of vanilla ice cream. Stir gently to combine, then finish with a sprinkling of matcha to garnish.

KUNZEA POMIFERA

The dry vermouth from Adelaide Hills Distillery is an interesting vermouth and quite aromatic. It has the perception of sweetness while being quite dry, with only 7 g (⅛ oz) per 1 litre (34 fl oz) of residual sugar. The hints of honey and wattleseed in this vermouth led me to use it in this cocktail, as the flavours help to bring out the 'apple pie' flavour of the native Australian muntries.

60 ml (2 fl oz) **Adelaide Hills Distillery dry vermouth**
2 tablespoons **Muntrie Jam** (page 72)
15 ml (½ fl oz) **lemon juice**
15 ml (½ fl oz) **egg white**
ice cubes, for shaking
dehydrated apple, to garnish

Combine all the ingredients except the ice in a cocktail shaker and shake vigorously for 10 seconds. Open the shaker and top with ice cubes, then shake for another 10 seconds.

Strain into a chilled Coupette glass and garnish with a slice of dehydrated apple.

TONIC OF ANTEROS

Anteros is the Greek god of passion and love, and I am passionate about Chinato and love Barolo Chinato. Cocchi's Barolo Chinato is an amazing example, and it works really well in this simple cocktail. Enjoy it with some bitter dark chocolate on the side, which will help to balance out the sweetness of the drink.

45 ml (1½ fl oz) Cocchi Barolo Chinato

5 ml (⅛ fl oz) grenadine

5 ml (⅛ fl oz) amaretto

dash of orange bitters

1 block rock ice

1 orange wedge, to garnish

1 square bitter dark chocolate, to serve

Combine all the ingredients except the ice in a chilled Old Fashioned glass and stir to mix. Add a block of rock ice and stir again, for 30 seconds, to chill and dilute the drink.

Garnish with an orange wedge and serve a square of bitter dark chocolate on the side.

QUINCE SOUR

A buddy of mine, Andy Griffiths, made me some quince paste this year, and it was so good it inspired this cocktail. Castagna's bianco vermouth has lovely honey aromatics, which are accentuated with a dash of rosewater.

45 ml (1½ fl oz) Castagna bianco vermouth

2 tablespoons quince paste

15 ml (½ fl oz) lemon juice

5 ml (⅛ fl oz) amaretto

dash of rosewater

4 drops InstaFoam (page 85)

ice cubes, for shaking

pickled walnuts, to garnish

Combine all the ingredients except the ice in a cocktail shaker and shake vigorously for 10 seconds. Open the shaker and top with ice cubes, then seal and shake for another 10 seconds.

Strain into a chilled Coupette glass and garnish with pickled walnuts.

SUMMER'S FUNERAL

□

This was the first Maidenii cocktail, written way back in 2012. Maidenii Classic vermouth works really well with the autumnal flavours of pomegranate and apple. Be sure to invest in real grenadine rather than red sugar syrup and, while the brittle isn't mandatory, it certainly is delightful to nibble on while drinking this cocktail on a chilly autumn evening.

30 ml (1 fl oz) Maidenii Classic vermouth
30 ml (1 fl oz) Calvados
15 ml (½ fl oz) grenadine
2 dashes of Angostura bitters
1 block rock ice
apple fan, to garnish (page 81)
Macadamia Brittle, to serve (page 73)

Combine all the ingredients except the ice in a chilled Old Fashioned glass and stir to mix. Add a block of rock ice and stir briefly, to chill and dilute the drink.

Garnish with an apple fan and serve with the brittle on the side.

NICK BELIEVES THE KEY TO A GOOD MORNING! IS THE WATTLESEED
△ SYRUP, WHICH BRINGS OUT THE SPICIER NOTES IN THE VERMOUTH.

GOOD MORNING!

(pictured opposite)

Possibly the best way to start the day: vermouth, coffee and a bacon sarnie. The coffee and Wattleseed Syrup in this recipe really bring out the spicier notes in the vermouth.

45 ml (1½ fl oz) **Cocchi Barolo Chinato**

5 ml (⅛ fl oz) **Wattleseed Syrup** (page 64)

45 ml (1½ fl oz) **Cold-brew Coffee** (see below)

ice cubes, to serve

1 bacon sarnie, to serve

COLD-BREW COFFEE (MAKES 1 LITRE/34 FL OZ)

75 g (2¾ oz) **freshly ground coffee beans**

1 litre (34 fl oz) **chilled filtered water**

To make the cold-brew coffee, combine the ground coffee and water in a bowl. Cover and leave to macerate for 12 hours.

Line a fine-mesh sieve with a piece of muslin (cheesecloth) and suspend it over a large bowl or jug. Strain the cold brew into the bowl, discarding the coffee grounds, then pour into a sterilised glass bottle (see page 78) and seal tightly. Store in the refrigerator for up to 1 week.

Make a Good Morning! by combining all the ingredients except the ice in a chilled teacup. Top with ice cubes and serve with a bacon sarnie on the side.

SMOKED SWIZZLE

Simple vermouth cocktails with limited ingredients can still be complex in flavour. I guess it has to do with the number of different botanicals used to make vermouth and, depending on the modifier, what accentuates the different notes in a botanical blend. Here, Edward Quatermass' use of yuzu really highlights the kaffir lime in the vermouth, and the honey brings out the spice.

60 ml (2 fl oz) **Maidenii dry vermouth**

15 ml (½ fl oz) **yuzu juice**

5 ml (⅛ fl oz) **smoked honey**

crushed ice

honeycomb slice and a burnt cinnamon stick, to garnish

Combine all the ingredients in a chilled julep cup and top with crushed ice. Mix everything together vigorously using a bar spoon.

Top with more crushed ice, then garnish with a honeycomb slice and a burnt cinnamon stick.

SLOW BYRNE

 SAM CURTIS

This cocktail was created at a Wild Harvest session, an event held to showcase and celebrate native Australian food and ingredients. This particular night, Maidenii did all the drink pairings. The team and I decided to create an aperitif-style cocktail using equal parts Cape Byron Distillery Brookie's 'Slow' gin (made with native Australian Davidson plums), and Maidenii dry and sweet vermouths. What started off as a sort of reverse Wet Martini morphed into a twist on a Negroni, and we named it after the Slow gin and Maidenii co-conspirator, Shaun Byrne. Ideally, this cocktail should be garnished with a fresh strawberry gum leaf, if you can find one.

30 ml (1 fl oz) **Maidenii dry vermouth**
30 ml (1 fl oz) **Maidenii sweet vermouth**
30 ml (1 fl oz) **Brookie's Slow gin**
ice cubes, for mixing
1 block rock ice, to serve
1 strawberry gum leaf, to garnish

Combine all the ingredients in a mixing glass and top with ice cubes. Stir, to chill and dilute, for about 20 seconds.

Add a block of rock ice to a chilled Old Fashioned glass and strain the cocktail over the top. Garnish with a strawberry gum leaf.

BREAKFAST
IN AUTUMN

 ANDY GRIFFITHS

Bright and textural, this low-alcohol pick-me-up is the perfect accompaniment to brunch to awaken the palate. The mildly bitter notes and lively botanicals in Maidenii dry vermouth work incredibly well with the citrus and floral ingredients. Egg white is thrown in to give the cocktail a lovely velvety texture, and there's a hint of salt for seasoning.

60 ml (2 fl oz) **Maidenii dry vermouth**
25 ml (¾ fl oz) **cold-pressed apple juice**
15 ml (½ fl oz) **Chamomile Syrup** (see below)
5 ml (⅛ fl oz) **egg white**
2 dashes of **Saline Solution** (page 77)
2 dashes of **Citric Solution** (page 77)
ice cubes, for shaking
1 **Spanish olive on a toothpick, to garnish**

CHAMOMILE SYRUP (MAKES APPROX. 300 ML/10 FL OZ)

10 g (¼ oz) **dried chamomile flowers**
300 g (10½ oz) **caster** (superfine) **sugar**

To make the chamomile syrup, fill a saucepan with 300 ml (10 fl oz) water and bring to the boil. Add the dried chamomile, reduce the heat to medium and simmer for 2 minutes.

Strain the water through a fine-mesh sieve into a clean bowl or saucepan, discarding the chamomile. Add the sugar and stir until dissolved, then pour into a sterilised glass bottle (see page 78) and seal tightly. Store in the refrigerator for up to 1 week.

For a Breakfast In Autumn, combine all the ingredients except the ice in a cocktail shaker and shake vigorously for 10 seconds. Open the shaker and top with the ice cubes, then seal and shake or another 10 seconds.

Strain into a chilled Coupette glass and garnish with a Spanish olive on a toothpick.

CASABLANCA

(pictured opposite)

I wrote this cocktail in 2014, when we discovered the local fruit and veg' shop was selling fresh turmeric. If you haven't used it before, it is incredible, with a huge amount of flavour, spice and colour. I served this cocktail at my wedding this year and it was, without a doubt, the most popular cocktail of the day.

30 ml (1 fl oz) Maidenii sweet vermouth
30 ml (1 fl oz) The Botanist gin
30 ml (1 fl oz) Turmeric Tisane (see below)
15 ml (½ fl oz) lime juice
45 ml (1½ fl oz) soda water (club soda)
ice cubes, to serve
Vietnamese mint sprig, to garnish

TURMERIC TISANE (MAKES APPROX. 400 ML/13½ FL OZ)

60 g (2 oz) fresh turmeric root
300 g (10½ oz) caster (superfine) sugar
30 g (1 oz) mint leaves

First, prepare the turmeric tissane. Peel and grate the turmeric (wear gloves, or you'll end up with bright-orange fingers). Combine the sugar with 300 ml (10 fl oz) hot water in a large bowl and stir until dissolved. Add the grated turmeric and mint leaves, cover, and leave to infuse for 1 hour.

Strain the syrup through a fine-mesh sieve into a sterilised glass bottle (see page 78) and seal tightly. Store in the refrigerator for up to 1 week.

To make a Casablanca, combine all the ingredients except the soda water and ice in a chilled Collins glass. Gently pour in the soda water and carefully top with ice cubes to retain the fizz. Serve garnished with a sprig of Vietnamese mint.

THE SUBCONTINENTAL

 SAMUEL NG

Based on the modern classic cocktail London Calling, this twist plays on the heavy cardamom notes of the spiced negroni, and the addition of fresh curry leaves gives it a lively spiciness. The name comes from the region where curry leaves and many other botanicals are found: the subcontinent.

20 ml (¾ fl oz) Maidenii dry vermouth
45 ml (1½ fl oz) Four Pillars Spiced Negroni gin
25 ml (¾ fl oz) lemon juice
5 ml (⅛ fl oz) 2:1 Sugar Syrup (page 77)
dash of orange bitters
4 fresh curry leaves
ice cubes, for shaking

Combine all the ingredients in a cocktail shaker and top with ice cubes. Shake vigorously for 10 seconds, then strain into a chilled Coupette glass and garnish with a curry leaf.

WINTER

As the weather gets cooler, it is time to drink richer, bolder and sometimes even warmer drinks.

Earthy flavours abound, freshened with seasonal citrus. I adore oranges in winter, and truffles are around this time of year too. Hard spices, such as nutmeg, cinnamon and allspice are perfect for adding depth to drinks.

At the vemouthery, we are in the final cycle of production during winter. We finalise blending and get the vermouth into bottles. It is also where the cycle starts all over again and we pick the botanicals for maceration.

RADICCHIO SPRITZO

(pictured opposite)

Fancy (bitter) lettuce may
not be the first thing that
comes to mind as a garnish for
your spritz, but it does work
incredibly well in this cocktail,
emphasising the citrus notes
of the Mancino.

45 ml (1½ fl oz) Mancino Bianco Ambrato vermouth

10 ml (¼ fl oz) orange liqueur

5 ml (⅛ fl oz) Suze

60 ml (2 fl oz) soda water (club soda)

ice cubes, to serve

rolled radicchio leaf, to garnish

Combine all the ingredients except the soda water in a chilled wine glass and
stir to mix. Gently pour in the soda water and carefully top with ice cubes to
retain the fizz. Garnish with a rolled radicchio leaf.

SQUEEZE THE AMERICANO

This is a really simple, refreshing
cocktail made using a sherbet,
which is an aromatic cordial
of sorts. The process of
making the syrup involves
an *oleo-saccharum* which,
translated from Latin, means
sugar oil. By keeping the zest
and the sugar together, the
sugar draws out the oils in the
zest making it quite, well, zesty.
Cocchi Americano is a good
match here with its gentian root
prominence that really speaks
to the zingy grapefruit.

60 ml (2 fl oz) Cocchi Americano vermouth

30 ml (1 fl oz) Citrus Sherbet (page 54)

15 ml (½ fl oz) verjus

60 ml (2 fl oz) soda water (club soda)

ice cubes, to serve

grapefruit wedge, to garnish

Combine the vermouth, sherbet and verjus in a chilled highball glass and
gently pour in the soda water. Top with ice cubes to retain the fizz and garnish
with a grapefruit wedge to serve.

NEW YORK TODDY

LOUDON COOPER

I came up with this drink in
the middle of winter as I was
making a lot of hot toddies.
At the time, I was using a lot of
dried spices – both fresh and
in a syrup – to get a deeper,
wintery aroma in the drink.
One busy night, I ran out of
spiced syrup and had to figure
out a way to replace it. In
the end, I decided to cross a
Manhattan, a New York Sour
and a Hot Toddy, and the result
was pretty interesting. I'm a
bit obsessed with using local
produce, so Maidenii was an
easy choice and a great source
of local flavours and aromatics.

20 ml (¾ fl oz) **Maidenii Classic vermouth**
45 ml (1½ fl oz) **rye whiskey**
15 ml (½ fl oz) **lemon juice**
10 ml (¼ fl oz) **Honey Syrup** (page 77)
grated lemon zest and star anise, to garnish

Combine all the ingredients in a teacup and stir to mix. Transfer to
the microwave and heat on high for 30 seconds, or until hot.

Garnish with a grating of lemon zest and a star anise.

DR TEQUILA

They say that honey is good
for you in moderation. In the
case of leatherwood honey – a
beautifully aromatic honey
from Tasmania – a little goes
a long way. It is great to use in
cocktails like this one, where
Maidenii quinquina meets
vegetal tequila, zingy citrus and
the spicy, floral honey.

20 ml (¾ fl oz) **Maidenii quinquina**
20 ml (¾ fl oz) **tequila**
60 ml (2 fl oz) **orange juice**
1 teaspoon **Leatherwood honey**
ice cubes, for shaking
thyme sprig, to garnish

Combine all the ingredients in a cocktail shaker and top with ice cubes.
Shake vigorously for 10 seconds, then strain into a chilled Coupette glass
and garnish with a thyme sprig.

DRY & DRY

 SEBASTIAN COSTELLO

My brother and his girlfriend (now wife) and I used to finish summer exams at Melbourne University, then go down to a restaurant called Jimmy Watson's for a couple of bottles of takeaway dry and dry. They would take a bottle out of the fridge, fill it one-third of the way with their own dry vermouth, then top it up with dry ginger post mix. It would then be wrapped in brown paper and we would drink it under a tree. Since then, it has been my go-to for the first drink of the day or just a casual start to an afternoon.

45 ml (1½ fl oz) **Maidenii dry vermouth**
90 ml (3 fl oz) **dry ginger ale**
ice cubes, to serve
orange wedge, to garnish
shell-on peanuts, to serve

Add the vermouth to a chilled highball glass, then gently pour in the ginger ale. Carefully top with ice cubes to retain the fizz, then garnish with an orange wedge and serve with a small bowl of peanuts in their shells.

PERIGORD COCKTAIL

The Perigord region of France is home to a number of decadent things, including foie gras and truffles, and this cocktail captures this decadence. Maidenii Nocturne is a bitter wine, similar to amaro, with just a wine base. One of its main botanicals is Yarra Valley black truffles. They really fill out the mouthfeel of the product and give the vermouth a strong backbone for the other flavours to work with.

10 ml (¼ fl oz) **Maidenii Nocturne vermouth**
30 ml (1 fl oz) **Foie Gras Brandy** (see below)
ice cubes, for mixing
shaved fresh black truffle, to garnish
foie gras on brioche, to serve

FOIE GRAS BRANDY (MAKES 150 ML/5 FL OZ)

100 g (3½ oz) **good-quality foie gras**
150 ml (5 fl oz) **very old cognac (XO minimum)**

Start by preparing the foie gras brandy. Sear the foie gras in a frying pan over medium–high heat for 5 minutes to render the fat.

Pour the foie gras fat and cognac into a bowl, discarding the solids. Cover and refrigerate for 12 hours, or overnight.

Line a fine-mesh sieve with a piece of muslin (cheesecloth), suspend over a large bowl and pour in the cognac. Leave to drain, then pour the foie gras brandy into a sterilised glass bottle (see page 78). Seal the bottle tightly and store in the refrigerator for up to 2 weeks.

To make a Perigord Cocktail, combine all the ingredients in a mixing glass and top with ice cubes. Stir to chill and dilute for about 20 seconds.

Strain into a chilled Nick & Nora glass and garnish with shaved fresh black truffle. Serve with foie gras on brioche on the side.

THE LAST PIECE OF THE PUZZLE IN AN EVE'S CHEAT DAY IS
THE CHOCOLATE BUTTER; IT TAKES THE DRINK FROM GOOD
△   TO UNBELIEVABLE! – TRISH BREW

EVE'S CHEAT DAY

(pictured opposite)

 TRISH BREW

I created this cocktail for the Bombay Sapphire Project Botanicals winter promotional event. I was assigned the grain of paradise spice and had to use this as a starting point to create the cocktail. When I began researching it, I discovered this spice was used in a hippocras, a spiced wine that can be served warm. You know what else is a spiced wine? That's right: vermouth. So I decided to combine the two, freshen it with some ginger beer and nuke it in the microwave. Don't skimp on the chocolate butter.

30 ml (1 fl oz) **Maidenii Classic vermouth**
30 ml (1 fl oz) **Bombay Sapphire gin**
30 ml (1 fl oz) **ginger beer**
1 × 5 mm (¼ in) **slice of Chocolate Butter, to garnish** (see below)

CHOCOLATE BUTTER (MAKES APPROX. 280 G/10 OZ)

250 g (9 oz) **salted butter**
20 g (¾ oz) **Valrhona cocoa powder**
20 g (¾ oz) **light brown sugar**

To make the chocolate butter, allow the butter to come to room temperature, then fold through the cocoa powder and sugar using a fork. Make sure the ingredients are evenly distributed.

Heap the butter into the middle of a piece of plastic wrap and roll into a log shape. Place it in the fridge until ready to use. The butter will keep in the refrigerator for up to 1 week.

Make an Eve's Cheat Day by combining all the ingredients in a teacup and stir to mix. Transfer to the microwave and heat on high for 30 seconds, or until hot.

Garnish with a slice of chocolate butter to serve.

SCOFFLAW

 JAMES CONNOLLY

This was the first shaken vermouth drink I fell in love with! I can remember the day I first tried it — it was at a bar called Low 302 in Sydney and the bartender, Rory, made me one of these because I had asked for 'something with rye'. It's been one of my favourite drinks ever since! Here is my version.

15 ml (½ fl oz) **Noilly Prat dry vermouth**
45 ml (1½ fl oz) **rye whiskey**
15 ml (½ fl oz) **grenadine**
25 ml (¾ fl oz) **lemon juice**
3 dashes of **orange bitters**
ice cubes, for shaking
lemon twist, to garnish

Combine all the ingredients in a cocktail shaker and top with ice cubes. Shake vigorously for 10 seconds, then strain into a chilled Coupette glass and garnish with a lemon twist.

FLAPJACKET #2

 CHRIS HYSTED-ADAMS

This cocktail featured on the first list we launched in our bar The Attic above Black Pearl in Melbourne. At the time, we were keen to offer super flavoursome, low-alcohol cocktails. For this drink, we were drawn to Dolin rouge for its delicate structure and full flavour. We used orgeat to enhance the mouthfeel and orange bitters to increase complexity. When the ice begins to melt into the liquid, the vermouth mingles with the tannins of the tea.

60 ml (2 fl oz) Dolin rouge vermouth

7 ml (⅛ fl oz) orgeat

2 dashes of orange bitters

3–4 large cubes Russian Caravan Tea Ice (see below)

1 spray Laphroaig Scotch whisky, to garnish

RUSSIAN CARAVAN TEA ICE (MAKES 1 LITRE/34 FL OZ)

50 g (1¾ oz) Russian Caravan tea leaves

1 litre (34 fl oz) filtered water

To make the Russian Caravan tea ice, combine the tea with the filtered water in a large bowl and leave to macerate for 1 hour.

Strain the tea through a fine-mesh sieve into a jug, discarding the tea leaves. Carefully pour the tea into ice-cube trays and freeze.

For a Flapjacket #2, combine all the ingredients in a chilled rocks glass and stir to mix. Add the Russian Caravan tea ice and stir gently for about 10 seconds. Garnish with a spray of smoky Laphroaig to serve.

BLOOD & SAND

SEBASTIAN RAEBURN

This crazy drink was created for the premier of the 1922 silent movie *Blood and Sand*. It was inspired by the 1908 book of the same name by Vincente Ibanez, and told the story of the rise and fall of a bullfighter. There is no record of who originally produced the drink, and it did not appear in print until 1930 when it was included in the *Savoy Cocktail Book*.

20 ml (¾ fl oz) Martini Riserva Rubino vermouth

20 ml (¾ fl oz) blended Scotch whisky

20 ml (¾ fl oz) cherry liqueur

20 ml (¾ fl oz) fresh orange juice

ice cubes, for shaking

orange twist, to garnish

Combine all the ingredients except the ice in a cocktail shaker and top with ice cubes. Shake vigorously for 10 seconds, then strain into a chilled Coupette glass and garnish with an orange twist.

BENEATH THE FASCINATOR

NICK TESAR

A variant of the classic Smoky Martini, this cocktail won the food and drink pairing in Australian competition Diageo's Be Braver With Flavour. It was paired with a dish of slippery mackerel in a chilli and mussel broth, with a salt and vinegar purple congo potato crisp on top. The starch in the gin amplified the richness of the mussel stock, while the smoky iodine elements of the whisky cut through the fish.

10 ml (¼ fl oz) Cocchi Vermouth di Torino
40 ml (1¼ fl oz) Potato Starch-washed Gin (see below)
10 ml (¼ fl oz) peated Scotch whisky
ice cubes, for mixing
lemon twist, to garnish

POTATO STARCH-WASHED GIN (MAKES 700 ML/23½ FL OZ)

70 g (2½ oz) purple congo potatoes
700 ml (23½ fl oz) Tanqueray No. 10 gin

To make the potato starch-washed gin, start by slicing the potatoes thinly on a mandoline. Rinse them under cold running water, then combine with the gin in a large bowl. Cover and leave to macerate for 1 hour.

Strain the gin through a fine-mesh sieve into a sterilised glass bottle (see page 78), discarding the potato. Seal the bottle tightly and store in the refrigerator for up to 2 months.

Make a Beneath The Fascinator by combining all the ingredients in a mixing glass and topping with ice cubes. Stir to chill and dilute for about 20 seconds.

Strain into a chilled Nick & Nora glass and garnish with a lemon twist.

INCITATION COCKTAIL

NICK TESAR

This cocktail was made for the opening of the ambitious restaurant Lûmé, in Melbourne. It is a full-flavoured, lower-alcohol drink, designed to awaken the senses prior to dining. The original cocktail was made by muddling the coriander (cilantro) in liquid nitrogen and serving it with a smoking piece of freeze-dried mandarin, but we've kept things a little simpler for this version.

30 ml (1 fl oz) Maidenii dry vermouth
30 ml (1 fl oz) amaro
30 ml (1 fl oz) Mandarin Shrub (see below)
4 coriander (cilantro) leaves, plus a coriander sprig to garnish
ice cubes, for shaking

MANDARIN SHRUB (MAKES APPROX. 800 ML/27 FL OZ)

750 g (1 lb 11 oz) whole mandarins
750 g (1 lb 11 oz) caster (superfine) sugar
750 ml (25½ fl oz) verjus

To prepare the shrub, peel the mandarins, reserving the peel and the fruit.

Combine the sugar, verjus and mandarin fruit and peel in a sealable plastic bag (ideally vacuum sealed). Seal the bag well, then shake and massage to dissolve the sugar and crush the fruit. Leave to macerate for 48 hours, then strain the mixture through a chinois, or very fine-mesh sieve, into a jug, pressing down on the fruit to extract as much juice as possible.

Pour the shrub into a sterilised glass bottle (see page 78) and seal tightly. Store in the refrigerator for up to 1 month.

Make an Incitation Cocktail by combining all the ingredients except the ice in a cocktail shaker. Top with ice cubes and shake vigorously for 10 seconds. Strain into a chilled Coupette glass and garnish with a coriander sprig.

PRE-DINNER

A cocktail before dinner is the best way to prepare the body for an onslaught of food.

Stimulating the appetite is a must, as is unwinding from the day. The ideal drink is either slightly bitter or something effervescent and lighter on the sugar, as sugar can coat the palate and make you feel full.

Some must-have ingredients for the back bar when preparing pre-dinner tipples are vermouth (of course), sherry (the drier the better), Champagne (over sparkling wine) and gin (lots and lots of gin). All of these items are great chilled on their own or can form the base for mixing great pre-dinner delights.

VERMOUTH BRINGS THE FUNK

(pictured opposite)

Kombucha, a fermented tea drink, has come into vogue over the past few years, with different brands popping up all over the place. Finding a good brand is key and I always prefer to use the unflavoured varieties as the flavoured ones tend to mask the other ingredients in a drink. Dolin Blanc is a light vermouth with a floral finish that gives the coconut water a lift.

60 ml (2 fl oz) Dolin Blanc vermouth

30 ml (1 fl oz) coconut water

pulp of ¼ fresh passionfruit

90 ml (3 fl oz) unflavoured kombucha

ice cubes, to serve

lemongrass stalk and passionfruit half, to garnish

Combine the vermouth, coconut water and passionfruit pulp in a chilled highball glass and stir to mix. Gently pour in the kombucha and carefully top with ice cubes to retain the fizz. Garnish with a lemongrass stalk and a passionfruit half.

GIN, WINE & TONIC

This is another cocktail from my time at Gin Palace in Melbourne. It was designed to refresh and stimulate, combining bitter, salty, sweet and tart flavours, and a gin kicker, of course. There aren't that many quinquinas on the market compared to vermouth, so this one hails from South Africa and is delightfully bitter with a lovely honeyed sweetness.

20 ml (¾ fl oz) Caperitif quinquina

40 ml (1¼ fl oz) gin

20 ml (¾ fl oz) manzanilla sherry

5 ml (⅛ fl oz) tonic syrup

dash of Citric Solution (page 77)

ice cubes, for mixing

lemon wedge, to garnish

olives on a toothpick, to serve

Combine all the ingredients in a mixing glass and top with ice cubes. Stir, to chill and dilute, for about 20 seconds.

Strain into a chilled Collins glass and garnish with a lemon wedge. Serve a toothpick of olives on the side.

TIP *You can purchase tonic syrup online at onlybitters.com.au.*

CHRYSANTHEMUM

 SEBASTIAN RAEBURN

In 1930, the SS Europa was launched from Germany. It was a passenger liner in the grand style, which ploughed the waves between Germany and New York for nearly a decade. As soon as the liner reached international waters out of New York, it was able to serve alcohol to the thirsty Americans struggling under the oppressive laws of Prohibition. One of the signature cocktails on board was the Chrysanthemum. This complex, zesty and potent beverage made it down through the decades and is still enjoyed today.

60 ml (2 fl oz) **Carpano dry vermouth**
30 ml (1 fl oz) **DOM Bénédictine**
5 ml (⅛ fl oz) **absinthe**
ice cubes, for mixing
orange twist, to garnish

Combine all the ingredients in a mixing glass and top with ice cubes. Stir, to chill and dilute, for about 20 seconds.

Strain into a chilled Coupette glass and garnish with an orange twist.

FRENCH SPRITZ #2

I created this cocktail for a piece in *Alquimie* magazine on aperitif cocktails. All of the ingredients are French and, as you can probably tell from the recipe name, this was my second French Spritz. A note on Lillet: if you can't find the reserve brand, feel free to use their regular version, but it is well worth hunting down the reserve, as it adds a decadent dimension to this cocktail.

20 ml (¾ fl oz) **Lillet Blanc Reserve 2008 vermouth**
20 ml (¾ fl oz) **Citadelle gin**
10 ml (¼ fl oz) **Suze**
40 ml (1¼ fl oz) **Champagne**
ice cubes, to serve
lemon twist, to garnish

Combine all the ingredients except the Champagne and ice in a chilled Burgundy wine glass and stir to mix. Gently pour in the Champagne and carefully top with ice cubes to retain the fizz. Garnish with a lemon twist to serve.

LA DISCO TONIQUE

 NICK TESAR

This was the last cocktail I made during my time at Melbourne restaurant Lûmé. Intended to be served before an evening's dining, it was a variation on the classic Bamboo cocktail, utilising a richer, nuttier sherry and the newly-released Maidenii quinquina. It was named for its alluring colour, which came from the blueberry verjus.

20 ml (¾ fl oz) **Maidenii quinquina**
20 ml (¾ fl oz) **Blueberry Verjus** (page 112)
20 ml (¾ fl oz) **Sanchez Romate Fino Perdido**
10 ml (¼ fl oz) **2:1 Sugar Syrup** (page 77)
1 block rock ice
lemon twist, to garnish

Combine all the ingredients except the ice in a chilled rocks glass and stir to mix. Add the rock ice stir to chill and dilute for about 30 seconds. Garnish with a lemon twist and serve.

FRANKIE'S APERITIF

While working at Gin Palace, we had a regular customer who subsequently became a good friend. His name is Francesco Fiorelli, an Italian gent' who managed a restaurant upstairs called Sarti. One evening, Francesco brought in his favourite liqueur, mirto, from his home country, Italy. It is made with the fruit from *Myrtus communis,* or common myrtle. He asked me to create a cocktail for him to ready his body for his pre-shift meal, and Frankie's aperitif was born.

15 ml (½ fl oz) **Maidenii sweet vermouth**
45 ml (1½ fl oz) **Malfy gin**
15 ml (½ fl oz) **mirto**
ice cubes, for mixing
absinthe, for rinsing
lemon twist, to garnish

Combine all the ingredients in a mixing glass and top with ice cubes. Stir to chill and dilute for about 20 seconds.

Strain into a chilled Coupette glass rinsed with absinthe (see page 78) and garnish with a lemon twist.

MARTINI

There are many, many different ways to make a Martini. The trick is to work out how you like it and this can only be done by experimenting. The recipe below is how I like to drink mine. You could call it a 50/50 Martini, as vermouth and gin have been used in equal measure. Below, I have included some variations on ingredients and garnishes so you can tweak this recipe to suit your taste.

45 ml (1½ fl oz) **Maidenii dry vermouth**
45 ml (1½ fl oz) **Tanqueray No. 10 gin**
ice cubes, for mixing
grapefruit twist, to garnish

Combine the ingredients in a mixing glass and top with ice cubes. Stir, to chill and dilute, for about 20 seconds. Strain into a chilled cocktail glass and garnish with a grapefruit twist.

FLAVOUR VARIATIONS

'I HAVE A SWEET TOOTH'
Try a Wet Martini that uses more vermouth and/or use a sweeter vermouth.

'I LIKE SAVOURY FLAVOURS'
Add 1 teaspoon olive brine to make a Dirty Martini.

'I'M NOT A HUGE FAN OF GIN'
Try vodka. It's not a traditional Martini, but it's still delicious.

'I LOVE GIN MORE THAN I LOVE VERMOUTH'
The vermouth-maker in me says shame on you, but the bartender in me says use less vermouth to make it a Dry Martini.

'I CAN'T DRINK TOO MUCH ALCOHOL'
Try a Reverse Martini, which is mostly vermouth and lighter on the gin.

GARNISH VARIATIONS

SOUR
Citrus twist, yuzu leaf, pickled onion, apple slice or finger lime 'caviar'.

SPICE
Dash of any bitters, absinthe rinse (see page 78), nasturtium leaf, pickled pepper or kaffir lime leaf.

SWEET
Blue cheese-stuffed date, strawberry slice, melon ball or rosella flower in syrup.

FRESH
Mint sprig, basil leaf, rose petal or lemon myrtle leaf.

SAVOURY
Olives on a toothpick, anchovies on a toothpick, thyme sprig, rosemary sprig, cherry tomato or marigold flower.

A MARTINI IS A VERY PERSONAL THING - SEBASTIAN RAEBURN &
△ DERVILLA MCGOWAN

BAMBOO

 HUGO LEECH

A classic and refined low-alcohol pre-dinner tipple that dates from the turn of the nineteenth century when a bartender in Yokohama, Japan, produced the drink to appease the thirst of his international – particularly American – guests who had a taste for cocktails that were not yet prevalent in Japan. This recipe is a beautiful rendition of the original: a cocktail that is far greater than the sum of its parts. The addition of bitters gives it an aromatic edge, while the sugar syrup lends a silky texture to this delicate drink.

30 ml (1 fl oz) **Maidenii dry vermouth**
30 ml (1 fl oz) **fino sherry**
5 ml (⅛ fl oz) **2:1 Sugar Syrup** (page 77)
dash of orange bitters
ice cubes, for mixing
orange twist, to garnish

Combine all the ingredients in a mixing glass and top with ice cubes. Stir, to chill and dilute, for about 20 seconds.

Strain into a chilled Nick & Nora glass and garnish with an orange twist.

GOLDEN MILE

 JOE JONES

This one's a bit of a newcomer to my aperitif repertoire. It is mainly driven by sherry and vermouth and made slightly bitter with Suze: something between a White Americano and a Tom Collins with less alcohol for those pacing themselves over a long night. For a heavier alternative, substitute the soda water (club soda) with a dry, crisp lager.

25 ml (¾ fl oz) **Cocchi Americano vermouth**
25 ml (¾ fl oz) **La Goya fino sherry**
15 ml (½ fl oz) **Suze**
20 ml (¾ fl oz) **lemon juice**
10 ml (¼ fl oz) **2:1 Sugar Syrup** (page 77)
crushed ice, for shaking
1 ice spear
30 ml (1 fl oz) **soda water** (club soda)
orange slice, to garnish

Combine all the ingredients except the ice spear and soda water in a cocktail shaker with a few pellets of crushed ice. Shake vigorously for 10 seconds, or until the ice has dissolved.

Strain into a Collins glass and add an ice spear. Gently top with soda water, then garnish with an orange slice.

CARE THREE

Alastair Walker of Caretaker in New Zealand has been making high-quality, classically styled drinks for as long as I can remember. Previously of The Everleigh in Melbourne, Alastair has an attention to detail in building layers of flavour that must be commended. In this cocktail, he has balanced vegetal tequila with the sweetness of the maraschino, tying both flavours together with a textural dry vermouth.

15 ml (½ fl oz) Yzaguirre dry vermouth
45 ml (1½ fl oz) Tromba blanco tequila
5 ml (⅛ fl oz) maraschino liqueur
ice cubes, for mixing
lime twist and a spritz of mezcal, to garnish

Combine all the ingredients in a mixing glass and top with ice cubes. Stir, to chill and dilute, for about 20 seconds.

Strain into a chilled Nick & Nora glass and garnish with a lime twist and a spritz of mezcal.

BLACK SPUR

 CHRIS HYSTED-ADAMS

For a long time at Black Pearl, Mark Leahy and I wanted to create a cocktail using only Australian-inspired ingredients. Punters regularly asked about the Four Pillars Shiraz gin, but we were keen to use it as an accentuating flavour. Ripe and filled with berry fruit, this unique gin helps to provide a backbone for the drink, and the Regal Rogue Wild rosé vermouth seemed to be the perfect base for this.

50 ml (1¾ fl oz) Regal Rogue Wild rosé vermouth
20 ml (¾ fl oz) Four Pillars Shiraz gin
5 ml (⅛ fl oz) 2:1 Sugar Syrup (page 77)
1 bar spoon Distillery Botanica Reverie absinthe
ice cubes, for mixing
grapefruit twist, to garnish

Combine all the ingredients in a mixing glass and top with ice cubes. Stir to chill and dilute for about 20 seconds.

Strain into a chilled Coupette glass and garnish with a grapefruit twist to serve.

POST-DINNER

After a big meal, it's time to sit back, relax and round out the evening with another drink.

It is an opportunity to swap your dessert for a sweet drink or something that will help you digest your meal.

To mix those post-dinner tipples, a few items are essential to have on hand in addition to a fridge full of vermouth. A selection of amari (bitter Italian liqueurs) are a must and are just as delicious on their own as in mixed drinks. Brandy, brandy, brandy – something I absolutely adore – is the quintessential post-dinner beverage, best served with a cigar. Finally, tea and coffee are cracking in cocktails or, of course, served on their own.

KING GEORGE SQUARE

(pictured opposite)

This cocktail comes from Edward Quatermass, a buddy of mine who lives in Brisbane. He left the naming of this drink up to me – not my strong suit! So I decided to keep it simple and name it after a beautiful public space in Brisbane that was named after King George V.

25 ml (¾ fl oz) **Maidenii sweet vermouth**
25 ml (¾ fl oz) **Plantation pineapple rum**
25 ml (¾ fl oz) **rye whiskey**
ice cubes, for mixing
absinthe, for rinsing
lemon twist, to garnish

Combine all the ingredients in a mixing glass and top with ice cubes. Stir, to chill and dilute, for about 20 seconds.

Strain into a chilled rocks glass rinsed with absinthe (see page 78) and garnish with a lemon twist.

BIJOU

 HUGH LEECH

The Bijou is an old classic cocktail whose name means 'jewel' in French and was inspired by three precious stones: diamonds (gin), rubies (vermouth) and emeralds (Green Chartreuse). Starting with delicate sweetness and finishing with herbaceous intensity, this is one of the great surprises of the cocktail world and makes a truly delightful after-dinner sipper.

30 ml (1 fl oz) **Adelaide Hills Distillery sweet vermouth**
40 ml (1¼ fl oz) **Adelaide Hills 78 Degrees gin**
20 ml (¾ fl oz) **Green Chartreuse**
dash of orange bitters
ice cubes, for mixing
lemon twist, to garnish

Combine all the ingredients in a mixing glass and top with ice cubes. Stir, to chill and dilute, for about 20 seconds.

Strain into a chilled Coupette glass and garnish with a lemon twist.

BLOODY AWESOME MANHATTAN

 CHRIS HYSTED-ADAMS

Unfortunately, we can't lay claim to this classic cocktail; it was created by a bloke named Harry Johnson in 1884. Story goes that Harry liked to add a splash of Curaçao to his Manhattan, but we've found that adding a splash of absinthe instead works just as well and gives better structure to the drink while enhancing the sweet profile of the Carpano Antica Formula vermouth.

45 ml (1½ fl oz) **Carpano Antica Formula vermouth**
45 ml (1½ fl oz) **rye whiskey**
3 ml (⅛ fl oz) **orange liqueur**
3 ml (⅛ fl oz) **absinthe**
3 ml (⅛ fl oz) **2:1 Sugar Syrup** (page 77)
ice cubes, for mixing
1 fresh cherry, to garnish

Combine all the ingredients in a mixing glass and top with ice cubes. Stir, to chill and dilute, for about 20 seconds.

Strain into a chilled Coupette glass and garnish with a fresh cherry.

CAFFÈ CORRETTO ALLA M&M

This cocktail comes from a friend of mine, Sebastien Derbomez, who is the Monkey Shoulder whisky ambassador in the United States. When he sent me this recipe I looked at the ingredients and thought surely vermouth won't play nice with these flavours. How wrong I was, Sebastien. I take my hat off to you – it's a cracking cocktail.

30 ml (1 fl oz) **Monkey Shoulder whisky**
30 ml (1 fl oz) **Maidenii dry vermouth**
30 ml (1 fl oz) **freshly brewed espresso**
15 ml (½ fl oz) **orgeat**
ice cubes, for shaking
grated nutmeg, to garnish

Combine all the ingredients in a mixing glass and add the ice cubes. Shake vigorously for 10 seconds to dilute the drink, then strain into a chilled Nick & Nora glass. Garnish with grated nutmeg.

VERMOUTH & TEA

The basis of this recipe is a milk punch, which combines citrus with milk. Now, that may sound strange, but there is method in the madness. Adding lemon juice to milk splits the milk into curds and whey. We then collect the whey and use it to give texture to the punch. Be sure to use good-quality milk for this recipe.

30 ml (1 fl oz) pre-chilled Maidenii sweet vermouth
120 ml (4 fl oz) Milk Punch (see below)
fresh strawberries and a shortbread biscuit, to serve

MILK PUNCH (MAKES APPROX. 600 ML/20½ FL OZ)

zest of 2 large oranges
250 ml (8½ fl oz) Melbourne Gin Company gin
500 ml (17 fl oz) good-quality full-cream (whole) milk
15 g (½ oz) uva dry-season tea
250 ml (8½ fl oz) lemon juice
150 g (5½ oz) caster (superfine) sugar

First, prepare the milk punch. Combine the orange zest and gin in a bowl, cover, and leave to macerate for 12 hours, or overnight.

Put the milk in a saucepan and warm gently over medium heat, for 3–4 minutes, until the milk is warm but not hot. Stir in the tea, remove from the heat and leave to infuse for 5 minutes.

In a bowl, combine the milk mixture, gin, lemon juice and sugar and stir until the sugar has dissolved. Leave to sit for 1 hour.

Line a fine-mesh sieve with a piece of muslin (cheesecloth) and suspend it over a bowl. Pour in the milk mixture and leave to strain. Discard the curds.

Pour the milk punch into a sterilised glass bottle (see page 78). Seal tightly and store in the refrigerator for up to 1 week.

To make a Vermouth & Tea, mix the milk punch with the pre-chilled vermouth and pour into a chilled teacup. Serve with fresh strawberries and a shortbread biscuit on the side.

CARTHUSIAN FLIP

SEBASTIAN RAEBURN

I designed this drink to achieve
two goals: one, to combine
ingredients that go well before
and after dinner, and two,
to explore texture. It started
with Chartreuse, as it gives
the drink a silky mouthfeel. It
then became a flip, with the
addition of an egg. Being an
after-dinner drink, the inclusion
of a smoky whisky seemed to
make sense, but it didn't quite
fit the bill. Instead, I opted
for a Scotch whisky with the
addition of some vermouth to
brighten it up and cut through
the heaviness of the drink.
The result was fantastic.

15 ml (½ fl oz) **Cinzano 1757 Rosso vermouth**

50 ml (1¾ fl oz) **Bowmore Legend 10-year-old Scotch whisky**

15 ml (½ fl oz) **Yellow Chartreuse**

5 ml (⅛ fl oz) **2:1 Sugar Syrup** (page 77)

1 whole egg

ice cubes, for shaking

a pinch of saffron threads and fresh nutmeg, to garnish

Combine all the ingredients in a cocktail shaker and top with ice cubes.
Shake vigorously for 10 seconds, then strain into a chilled tulip glass and
garnish with a pinch of saffron threads and a grating of fresh nutmeg.

MAE KLONG EXPRESS

JAMES CONNOLLY

Named after the famous railway
market in Thailand, this drink is
a tequila-spiked, Thai-inspired
twist on one of my favourite
drinks, the Twentieth Century.
White cacao and chilli are
obvious partners in crime for
the blanco tequila, and the
Americano brings a complexity
and herbal element that is
missing from the original. It's a
pretty banging drink that fits a
multitude of occasions. If you
want to crank it up a notch,
reach for the mezcal.

25 ml (¾ fl oz) **Cocchi Americano vermouth**

25 ml (¾ fl oz) **Tromba Reposado tequila**

25 ml (¾ fl oz) **Chilli Cacao** (see below)

25 ml (¾ fl oz) **lemon juice**

3 dashes of orange bitters

dash of Saline Solution (page 77)

ice cubes, for shaking

lemon twist, to garnish

CHILLI CACAO (MAKES 350 ML/12 FL OZ)

350 ml (12 fl oz) **Mozart white crème de cacao**

10 g (¼ oz) **red bird's eye chilli, destemmed and roughly chopped**

Start by making the chilli cacao. Combine the crème de cacao and chilli in a
bowl, cover, and leave to macerate for 2 hours.

Strain through a fine-mesh sieve into a sterilised glass bottle (see page 78),
discarding the chilli. Seal tightly and store in the refrigerator for up to
2 months.

To make a Mae Klong Express, combine all the ingredients in a cocktail shaker
and top with ice cubes. Shake vigorously for 10 seconds, then strain into a
chilled Coupette glass and garnish with a lemon twist.

CORNER POCKET

 JOE JONES

A slightly post-tiki, low-alcohol drink – rich and tropical!

25 ml (¾ fl oz) **Dolin dry vermouth**
25 ml (¾ fl oz) **amaro Montenegro**
40 ml (1¼ fl oz) **pineapple juice**
20 ml (¾ fl oz) **lime juice**
15 ml (½ fl oz) **orgeat**
crushed ice, for shaking
1 **ice spear**
30 ml (1 fl oz) **soda water** (club soda)
lime wedge and pineapple leaf, to garnish

Combine all the ingredients except the ice spear and soda water in a cocktail shaker with a few pellets of crushed ice. Shake vigorously for 10 seconds, or until the ice has dissolved.

Strain into a chilled Collins glass and add an ice spear. Gently pour in the soda water and garnish with a lime wedge and a pineapple leaf.

COSMO-TINI

(pictured opposite)

This cocktail is a mash-up of two very popular cocktails: the Cosmopolitan and the Martini. The martini ingredients are there in plain sight, but the cosmo ingredients are hiding in the shrub.

40 ml (1¼ fl oz) **La Quintinye dry vermouth**
40 ml (1¼ fl oz) **Four Pillars Rare dry gin**
20 ml (¾ fl oz) **Cranberry Shrub** (see below)
ice cubes, for mixing
orange twist, to garnish

CRANBERRY SHRUB (MAKES 400 ML/13½ FL OZ)

250 g (9 oz) **dried cranberries**
250 g (9 oz) **caster** (superfine) **sugar**
250 ml (8½ fl oz) **apple-cider vinegar**

To make the cranberry shrub, combine all the ingredients in a saucepan with 250 ml (8½ fl oz) water and bring to the boil. Reduce the heat to medium and simmer for 30 minutes, stirring occasionally.

Strain the shrub through a fine-mesh sieve into a sterilised glass jar or bottle (see page 78), discarding the dried cranberries. Seal tightly and store in the refrigerator for up to 1 month.

For a Cosmo-tini, combine all the ingredients in a mixing glass and top with ice cubes. Stir, to chill and dilute, for about 20 seconds.

Strain into a chilled cocktail glass and garnish with an orange twist.

FILTHY MARTINEZ

  ANDY GRIFFITHS

Inspired by a trip to Spain where I discovered (in wonderment) vermouth on tap and pickled snacks! Creating a filthy version of the Martinez (a favourite of mine), was inevitable. Add to that my love of mezcal and sherry and the result was a punchy, aromatic and complex tipple that is perfect for serving with an array of Spanish tapas, such as cured meats, anchovies and assorted pickles. Casa Mariol *vermut* was the perfect choice here for its low caramel content and general herbaceousness.

1 **rosemary sprig**
1 **caper berry**
30 ml (1 fl oz) **Casa Mariol vermut negre**
40 ml (1¼ fl oz) **mezcal**
10 ml (¼ fl oz) **Oloroso sherry**
dash of orange bitters
ice cubes

1 **caper berry, to garnish**

Add the rosemary sprig to a mixing glass and scorch briefly with a flame. Add the caper berry and muddle with the rosemary until slightly crushed.

Add the remaining ingredients and top with ice cubes. Stir, to chill and dilute, for about 20 seconds.

Strain into a chilled Coupette glass and garnish with the caper berry, to serve.

BITTER

Bitter cocktails are an acquired taste; you have to train your palate to accept the intense flavours.

Always good before a meal, after a meal and, well, anytime you want to have a drink really. A variety of vermouths is a must when making bitter cocktails, but there are some other essentials too. Campari and Aperol are two of the most important – Aperol for those learning to like bitter flavours, and Campari for those who love them. There are also some great liqueurs in this style being made in Australia, including Okar and The Italian, both by producers in the Adelaide Hills. The other is Fernet, which is not for the faint-hearted, being so intensely bitter. My favourite brand is Branca.

VERMOUTH FLIP

(pictured opposite)

Flips are cocktails that contain a whole egg, and cacao nib antica is the perfect match. The heavy vanilla characters of the vermouth combined with cacao nibs give a real richness to this cocktail, while the Fernet-Branca gives it a bitter edge and a savoury, menthol influence. A great substitute for dessert.

50 ml (1¾ fl oz) **Cacao Nib Antica** (see below)

10 ml (¼ fl oz) **Fernet-Branca**

10 ml (¼ fl oz) **Canadian maple syrup**

1 whole **egg**

ice cubes, for shaking

fresh nutmeg, to garnish

CACAO NIB ANTICA (MAKES 750 ML/25½ FL OZ)

750 ml (25½ fl oz) **Carpano Antica Formula vermouth**

50 g (1¾ fl oz) **cacao nibs**

Start this recipe three days ahead.

First, prepare the cacao nib antica. Combine the vermouth and cacao nibs in a sealable bag (ideally vacuum sealed). Leave to macerate for 3 days.

Strain through a fine-mesh sieve into a sterilised glass bottle (see page 78), discarding the cacao nibs. Seal tightly and store in the refrigerator for up to 2 weeks.

To make a Vermouth Flip, combine all the ingredients in a cocktail shaker and top with ice cubes. Shake vigorously for 10 seconds, then strain into a chilled wine glass and garnish with freshly grated nutmeg.

YUZU COBBLER

This cocktail comes from Max Heart who heads up the bar Mjølner in Melbourne. I really like yuzu, though a little bit goes a long way. It certainly works to bring both the citrus and herbal flavours together seamlessly.

30 ml (1 fl oz) **Maidenii Classic vermouth**

20 ml (¾ fl oz) **Aperol**

20 ml (¾ fl oz) **vodka**

5 ml (⅛ fl oz) **Honey Syrup** (page 77)

3 dashes of **Dr Elmegirab's dandelion and burdock bitters**

crushed ice

30 ml (1 fl oz) **Capi yuzu soda**

lemon wedge and a **shisho leaf**, to garnish

Combine all the ingredients except the yuzu soda in a chilled wine glass and top with crushed ice. Mix vigorously with a bar spoon until well combined.

Top with the yuzu soda and garnish with a lemon wedge and a shisho leaf.

CHERRY & THE BEAN

Most people would be familiar with the coffee bean, but few would be familiar with the cherry of the coffee bean, which when dried is called cascara. I love using it to make an iced tea. Simply macerate the cascara in some water and add sugar and lemon to taste. The Cappelletti Chinato – an amazing Chinato with a lot of depth – gives this cocktail body and texture.

45 ml (1½ fl oz) **Cappelletti Chinato**
5 ml (⅛ fl oz) **freshly-brewed espresso**
45 ml (1½ fl oz) **Iced Cascara** (see below)
5 ml (⅛ fl oz) **kirsch**
ice cubes, to serve
Fabbri cherries, to garnish

ICED CASCARA (MAKES APPROX. 1.2 LITRES/41 FL OZ)

50 g (1¾ oz) **cascara**
150 g (5½ oz) **caster** (superfine) **sugar**

To make the iced cascara, put the cascara in a large bowl and cover with 1.2 litres (41 fl oz) water. Leave to macerate for 2 hours.

Strain the liquid through a fine-mesh sieve into a clean bowl and add the sugar. Stir until the sugar has dissolved, then pour into a sterilised glass bottle (see page 78), discarding the cascara. Seal tightly and store in the refrigerator for up to 1 week.

For a Cherry & The Bean, combine all the ingredients except the ice in a chilled highball glass and stir to mix. Top with ice cubes and garnish with Fabbri cherries.

TIP *You can source cascara directly from good coffee roasters.*

SUNBURNT

The story of this cocktail began when I was growing up and we used to have 12-pack bottles of soft drink delivered every week. The flavours were assorted and my favourite was portello, which is essentially a grape soda. Drinking it reminds me of my childhood and it works extremely well in place of soda water (club soda) in this Americano riff.

30 ml (1 fl oz) **Maidenii sweet vermouth**
15 ml (½ fl oz) **Applewood Okar**
2 dashes of **Citric Solution** (page 77)
60 ml (2 fl oz) **portello**
ice cubes, to serve
lemon myrtle sprig, to garnish

Combine all the ingredients except the portello and ice in a chilled highball glass. Gently pour in the portello and carefully top with ice cubes to retain the fizz.

Garnish with a sprig of lemon myrtle to serve.

IMPROVED
HANKY PANKY

 SAMUEL NG

I collaborated with Maidenii to create this cocktail, the Improved Hanky Panky. They produce a wonderful French-style amer called Nocturne, flavoured with local ingredients including the Yarra Valley black truffle. We were fortunate enough to be able to age our Navy Strength gin in a barrel that had previously held Maidenii Nocturne. We then finished it in 40-year-old sweet sherry barrels for 1 month. When we played around with the resulting gin, the cocktail that immediately came to mind was the Hanky Panky. To brighten up the palate a little, we added a touch of Pernod absinthe, and the Improved Hanky Panky was born.

40 ml (1¼ fl oz) **Maidenii sweet vermouth**

20 ml (¾ fl oz) **Four Pillars Navy Strength gin**

5 ml (⅛ fl oz) **Fernet-Branca**

absinthe, for rinsing (see page 78)

ice cubes, for mixing

1 block rock ice, to serve

orange twist, to garnish

Combine all the ingredients in a mixing glass and top with ice cubes. Stir, to chill and dilute, for about 20 seconds.

Rinse a chilled Old Fashioned glass with absinthe, then strain in the cocktail over a piece of rock ice and garnish with an orange twist.

NEGRONI

What a cocktail! I know it's certainly one of my favourites. We actually used this cocktail as a template when we developed our Maidenii sweet vermouth to make sure it would work perfectly in a Negroni. Four Pillars also developed their gin with the Negroni in mind. For something different, try replacing the Campari with other aperitifs – Okar is a great Australian option from Applewood Distillery in South Australia, as is The Italian from Adelaide Hills Distillery. Here is a really great, classic Negroni, but I have given some ideas for variations below too.

30 ml (1 fl oz) **Maidenii sweet vermouth**
30 ml (1 fl oz) **Four Pillars Spiced Negroni gin**
30 ml (1 fl oz) **Campari**
1 block rock ice
orange twist, to garnish

Build all the ingredients in a chilled Old Fashioned glass over a block of rock ice. Stir to chill and dilute for 30 seconds. Garnish with an orange twist to serve.

FLAVOUR VARIATIONS

'I DON'T LIKE BITTER DRINKS.'
Have a Gateway Negroni instead, with sloe gin instead of regular gin and Aperol instead of Campari.

'DO YOU HAVE A SOFTER VERSION OF A NEGRONI? I'M DRIVING.'
Try an Americano, which uses soda water (club soda) instead of gin.

'I DON'T LIKE THE RED COLOUR.'
Try a White Negroni, with Suze in place of Campari and Cocchi Americano in place of Maidenii.

'I LIKE BOURBON.'
Then a Boulevardier is what you want. Swap the gin for bourbon.

'DO YOU HAVE A MORE REFRESHING VERSION OF A NEGRONI?'
Go for a Sbagliato where the gin is subbed out for sparkling wine.

'WHAT IS A NEGRONI AUSTRALIS?'
An all-Australian Negroni, of course. Swap the Campari for Okar.

PURISTS WILL TELL YOU THAT A NEGRONI ISN'T A NEGRONI
WITHOUT CAMPARI, BUT YOU CAN REPLACE IT WITH A NUMBER
△ OF OTHER APERITIFS – CHRIS HYSTED-ADAMS

THREE-AND-A-HALF INGREDIENTS

(pictured opposite)

Punt e Mes vermouth is so named because its 'point and a half' represents one point of sweetness and half a point of bitterness. It is certainly on the richer, more bitter side of vermouth and I have found it works quite well in beer cocktails. Here, I've mixed it with one of my favourite stouts from Holgate, which is located close to our vermouthery in Harcourt and makes a perfect stop on the way home after spending the day elbow-deep in botanicals.

30 ml (1 fl oz) Punt e Mes vermouth
10 ml (¼ fl oz) Pedro Ximénez
90 ml (3 fl oz) Holgate Temptress stout
wasabi peanuts, to serve

Combine the vermouth and Pedro Ximénez in a highball glass. Gently top with beer and serve with wasabi peanuts.

THE OLD PAL

 SEBASTIAN RAEBURN

Published in Harry MacElhone's *ABC of Cocktails* in 1922, this cocktail was definitely inspired by drinks like the Negroni and Manhattan. It is very similar to an extra-bitter, ultra-dry Manhattan, but with a greater emphasis on the dark flavours of the rye.

20 ml (¾ fl oz) Noilly Prat dry vermouth
40 ml (1¼ fl oz) Bulleit rye whiskey
20 ml (¾ fl oz) Campari
ice cubes, for mixing
lemon twist, to garnish

Combine all the ingredients in a mixing glass and top with ice cubes. Stir to chill and dilute for about 20 seconds.

Strain into a chilled Coupette glass and garnish with a lemon twist.

LIVELY SPRITZER

This is one of Mark Ward's signature cocktails for his Regal Rogue Lively white vermouth, which is more of a bianco style with some lovely citrus notes balanced by savoury native thyme. It's a cracking drink to have during aperitivo – just remember to try and source White Marsh grapefruits, as these are the most bitter.

45 ml (1½ fl oz) **Regal Rogue Lively white vermouth**
15 ml (½ fl oz) **St Germain**
15 ml (½ fl oz) **White Marsh grapefruit juice**
dash of orange bitters
60 ml (2 fl oz) **prosecco**
ice cubes, to serve

grapefruit wedge, to garnish

Combine all the ingredients except the prosecco and ice in a chilled wine glass and stir to mix. Gently pour in the prosecco and carefully top with ice cubes to retain the fizz. Garnish with a grapefruit wedge to serve.

SPRITZ

This cocktail has grown in popularity in recent years and I can completely understand why. When the weather heats up, all I want to do is drink spritz during aperitivo! A spritz is made up of three main ingredients: wine, something bitter and something bubbly, usually soda water (club soda). Those are the only rules, which goes to show that you can make a spritz out of pretty much anything. Vermouth fulfils two of these requirements, being made of wine and being slightly bitter, so a vermouth and soda is actually a vermouth spritz. Here is my favourite recipe, but I have given some variations too so you can mix it up – literally.

60 ml (2 fl oz) **Maidenii Classic vermouth**
30 ml (1 fl oz) **prosecco**
15 ml (½ fl oz) **soda water** (club soda)
ice cubes, to serve
orange wedge, to garnish

Gently combine all the ingredients except the ice in a chilled Burgundy glass and stir to mix. Top with ice cubes to retain the fizz, then garnish with an orange wedge.

VARIATIONS

'IT'S SPRINGTIME, DO YOU HAVE SOMETHING FLORAL?'
Add a dash of orange-blossom water or rosewater.

'BERRIES ARE MY FAVOURITE.'
Add 15 ml (½ fl oz) Cassis and garnish with strawberries.

'I LIKE A SPRITZ, BUT I'VE HAD A ROUGH DAY AND NEED SOMETHING STRONGER.'
Why not add some gin? 30 ml (1 fl oz) should do it.

'I LOVE CIDER.'
Swap out the prosecco for a dry cider.

'I REALLY LIKE BITTER FLAVOURS.'
Use Punt e Mes instead of Maidenii Classic vermouth, or just add a couple of dashes of your favourite orange bitters.

AMERICOLA

Michael Chiem of PS40 in Sydney developed this recipe, which is a take on the Americano using his amazing wattleseed cola. It's available to purchase at his bar, but if you cannot get hold of it (you're missing out!) a good substitute would be 10 ml (¼ fl oz) of Wattleseed Syrup (page 64) mixed with 50 ml (1¾ fl oz) of your favourite cola.

30 ml (1 fl oz) Cocchi Vermouth di Torino
30 ml (1 fl oz) Campari
60 ml (2 fl oz) wattleseed cola or cola of your choice
1 block rock ice
orange wedge, to garnish

Combine all the ingredients except the cola and ice in a chilled Old Fashioned glass and stir to mix. Gently top with cola and carefully add a block of rock ice to retain the fizz. Stir again briefly, then garnish with an orange wedge.

LAC LEMAN

This is another cocktail from Alastair Walker of Caretaker in New Zealand. It is a beautifully refreshing highball, with a good kick of gentian. The Cocchi Americano, with its gentian bitterness and orange richness, is amplified by the gentian notes in the Suze. It is all rounded out by a sophisticated aromatic finish of fennel and anise with the addition of absinthe.

45 ml (1½ fl oz) Cocchi Americano vermouth
30 ml (1 fl oz) Suze
2 dashes of absinthe
100 ml (3½ fl oz) soda water (club soda)
ice cubes, to serve
lemon twist, to garnish

Combine all the ingredients except the soda water and ice to a chilled highball glass. Gently pour in the soda water and carefully top with ice cubes to retain the fizz.

Garnish with a lemon twist to serve.

PUNCH

Punch should be consumed with friends, which is one of the reasons it is considered bad luck to serve yourself!

Punch ingredients are many and varied. It is the drink of celebration, which leads people to want to come up with their own creations. A general rule of thumb for mixing punches is

1 part bitter
2 parts sweet
3 parts sour
4 parts strong
5 parts weak

The bitter in this equation could be vermouth, amaro or cocktail bitters – really, anything that's quite bitter. Sweetness can be brought in using liqueurs or syrups, and sour usually means citrus, but dry wines also work, as well as the juice of pomegranates, cranberries and apples. Any spirits will do for your strong element, but my favourites are gin and brandy. Finally, the weak element is usually a soft drink such as soda water (club soda), chilled tea or water. Essentially, anything that will take the edge off and make you want to keep going back for more.

SHERBET PUNCH

(pictured opposite and overleaf)

When I first wrote and tested this recipe, I thought it was OK, but it was certainly lacking in something. Enter one of my favourite cocktail ingredients: tea. When used correctly, tea can bring amazing subtlety to cocktails and punch and gives them some backbone, allowing other flavours to pop. Once I added the tea, the Cocchi rosa seemed to stand out and you could really notice the bitter cinchona bark of the Maidenii quinquina. Very quickly, this punch went from simple to superstar status.

SERVES 12

300 ml (10 fl oz) **Cocchi Americano rosa vermouth**
300 ml (10 fl oz) **Maidenii quinquina**
200 ml (7 fl oz) **Melbourne Gin Company gin**
100 ml (3½ fl oz) **St Germain**
200 ml (7 fl oz) **Black Tea Syrup** (page 103)
500 ml (17 fl oz) **soda water** (club soda)
300 ml (10 fl oz) **prosecco**
punch ice
marigold flowers, strawberries and mint sprigs, to garnish
soft cheese and fresh baguettes, to serve (optional)

Combine all the ingredients except the soda water, prosecco and punch ice in a large chilled punch bowl. Pour in the soda water and prosecco and top with a large piece of punch ice.

Garnish with marigold flowers, strawberries and mint sprigs, and serve some soft cheese and fresh baguettes alongside if desired. Serve in chilled punch glasses or wine glasses.

MULLED VERMOUTH

During winter, a refreshing punch isn't the first thing that springs to mind. However, I often find myself craving a rich-textured, warm punch when it's cold. I suggest that you make this recipe in advance, pour it into a thermos and take it on a winter picnic. Carpano Antica Formula is one of the richest vermouths out there, and it pairs perfectly with the spicy flavours in this punch. Don't skimp on the chocolate butter; it really makes the drink.

SERVES 8

400 ml (13½ fl oz) **Cacao Nib Antica** (page 172)
200 ml (7 fl oz) **Irish whiskey**
100 ml (3½ fl oz) **Wattleseed Syrup** (page 64)
100 ml (3½ fl oz) **Orange Curaçao**
100 ml (3½ fl oz) **amaro**
1 litre (34 fl oz) **boiling water**
50 g (1¾ oz) **Chocolate Butter** (page 145)
5 g (⅛ oz) **sea salt**
clove-studded orange zest and freshly grated nutmeg, to garnish
bitter chocolate and roasted almonds, to serve

Combine all the ingredients in a large saucepan and set over medium heat. Stir and warm gently for 5 minutes, or until hot. Pour the mulled vermouth into a thermos to keep warm.

When you're ready to serve, pour it into teacups and garnish with a piece of clove-studded orange zest and some freshly grated nutmeg. Serve with some bitter chocolate and roasted almonds on the side.

MAGNUM OF PUNCH

I actually created this punch recipe for my birthday one year. We rented a house in the country and I wanted to serve a celebratory punch to our guests on their arrival but, being on holiday, I didn't want to have to make it while I was away. The obvious solution was to make it at home and bring it with us. A usual wine bottle wouldn't suffice, so the Magnum of Punch was born. Maidenii Classic vermouth really enhances the autumn flavours in this punch, especially the earthy turmeric and zingy pomegranate.

SERVES 10

450 ml (15 fl oz) **Maidenii Classic vermouth**
200 ml (7 fl oz) **brandy**
500 ml (17 fl oz) **apple cider**
200 ml (7 fl oz) **Turmeric Tisane** (page 134)
150 ml (5 fl oz) **lemon juice**
ice cubes, to serve
seeds of 1 pomegranate, to garnish
Macadamia Brittle, to serve (page 73)

Combine all the ingredients except the ice in a large jug and carefully pour the mixture into a chilled magnum wine bottle or two normal wine bottles.

To serve, add ice cubes and pomegranate seeds to chilled wine glasses and pour in the punch. Serve with chunks of brittle on the side.

SUMMER OF VERMOUTH

This is a fun summer punch that Nick Tesar and I came up with while trying to create a punch with watermelon juice. It's so easy to make – just scoop out the watermelon flesh from the watermelon you will eventually use to hold the punch and blitz it in a food processor. Pass it through a fine-mesh sieve and you're ready to go. To make your watermelon vessel, cut one third off the top of the watermelon, then cut the smaller piece in half, scoop out the flesh and you have a perfect stand for your watermelon to sit on. Tequila and watermelon are a match made in heaven, and the undeniable wormwood fragrance of Absentroux brings the whole thing together.

SERVES 10

500 ml (17 fl oz) **Absentroux vermouth**
300 ml (10 fl oz) **Tromba blanco tequila**
250 ml (8½ fl oz) **Blueberry Verjus** (page 112)
750 ml (25½ fl oz) **freshly puréed watermelon juice**
150 ml (5 fl oz) **lime juice**
250 ml (8½ fl oz) **ginger beer**
punch ice, to serve
basil leaves, mint leaves and blueberries, to garnish

Combine all the ingredients in the hollowed-out watermelon and top with a large piece of punch ice. Garnish with basil, mint leaves and blueberries. Serve in chilled wine glasses.

VERMOUTH CATEGORIES

EXTRA DRY(<30 G/L)	DRY (<50 G/L)	MEDIUM DRY (>50 <90 G/L)	SWEET (>130 G/L)
Adelaide Hill Distillery dry	Belsazar dry	Adelaide Hills Distillery rosé	Belsazar red
Castagna Classic dry	Castagna bianco	Adelaide Hills Distillery rosso	Belsazar white
Causes & Cures semi-dry white	Drapo dry	Belsazar rosé	Carpano Antica Formula
Dolin dry	Margan off dry 15	Golfo tinto old vines	Cocchi Storico di Torino
La Quintinye extra-dry	Mulassano dry	La Quintinye royal blanc	Contratto rosso
Maidenii dry	Noilly Prat original dry	Lacuesta	Dolin blanc
Mancino secco	Riserva Carlo Alberto white	Maidenii Classic	Dolin rouge
Miro extra-dry	Reid+Reid dry vermouth	Margan off sweet 16	Drapo rosso
Mount Edward		Skew vermouth	Iris rojo
Oscar 697 extra-dry		Yzaguirre rojo clásico	La Quintinye rouge
Ransom dry		Regal Rogue Bold red	Maidenii sweet
Ravensworth Outlandish Claims bitter tonic		Regal Rogue Lively white	Mancino bianco ambrato
Regal Rogue Daring dry		Regal Rogue Wild rosé	Martini gran lusso
Riserva Carlo Alberto extra-dry		Yellow vermouth	Miro rojo
Uncouth Apple mint			Mulassano rosso
Vya extra-dry			Noilly Prat ambre
Vya whisper dry			Noilly Prat rouge
			Oscar 697 bianco
			Oscar 697 rosso
			Ransom sweet
			Riserva Carlo Alberto red
			Vergano
			Vermouth del Professore classico
			Vya sweet
			Yzaguirre blanco classico
			Yzaguirre rojo reserva

QUINQUINA (CINCHONA)	AMERICANO (GENTIAN)
Byrrh	Cocchi Americano
Cap Corse	Maidenii Long Chim Americano
Caperitif	
Dubonnet	
Lillet blanc	
Lillet rosé	
Maidenii La Tonique	
Rinquinquin	
St Raphael	

VERMOUTH CHINATO	AMARO
Bartolo Mascarello Barolo	Cocchi Dopo Teatro
Ceretto Barolo	Maidenii Nocturne
Cocchi Barolo	Mancino rosso amaranto
G. Borgogno Barolo	
G. Cappellano Barolo	
G. Conterno Barolo	
Gancia Antica ricetta Barolo	
Mancino Chinato	
Marcarini Barolo	
Mauro Vergano Barolo	
Roagna Barolo	
Mauro Vergano Chinato	

CONTRIBUTORS

To write this book we needed support from various experts, namely botanists, winemakers, chefs, bartenders, sommeliers and distillers. We have learned so much from these people while writing this book and, hopefully, you can learn something new too.

THE BOTANISTS

JUDE MAYALL

Jude Mayall is the owner of OutbackChef, a leading supplier and manufacturer of Australian native food products, and an industry advocate, educator, author and speaker on Australian native food. She has been actively involved with Australian Indigenous culture and native Australian botanicals for more than 30 years.

TIM ENTWISLE

Professor Tim Entwisle is a scientist, scientific communicator and botanic gardens director, and currently President of the International Association of Botanic Gardens (IABG). He was appointed Director and Chief Executive of the Royal Botanic Gardens Victoria in March 2013, following two years in a senior role at Royal Botanic Gardens Kew, and eight years as Executive Director of the Royal Botanic Gardens and Domain Trust in Sydney. Tim writes for a variety of science, nature and garden magazines and maintains an active social media profile (including his popular 'Talkingplants' blog). He contributes regularly to radio, including ABC RN *Blueprint for Living*, and hosted *Talking Plants* and co-hosted *In Season*.

THE BARTENDERS

ALASTAIR WALKER

Alastair is part owner of Caretaker bar in Auckland, New Zealand with his wife Heather Garland. Before moving to New Zealand, Alastair ran The Everleigh in Melbourne, where he was lucky enough to have been trained by Sasha Petraske and Michael Madrusan.

ANDY GRIFFITHS

Creative genius for the Speakeasy Group, Andy is a global award-winning bartender and experimental chef. He is known for his passion for fine food, craft beer, well-constructed drinks, spirited bartenders and splendid company.

NICK TESAR

Nick Tesar moved to Melbourne from Brisbane in 2013 and slotted easily into the team at Gin Palace, a Melbourne institution and late-night gin haunt. He spent two years there, where he felt he matured greatly as a bartender. He then took up the role of Bar Manager for the opening of fine dining restaurant Lûmé, in South Melbourne. In 2017, Marionette Liqueur was born with the help of long-time friends and colleagues Hugh, Lauren and Shaun. As well as spending time at Bad Frankies (on both sides of the bar!), he is now based at Fitzroy's Bar Liberty.

CAMILLE RALPH VIDAL

Bartender-turned-brand-ambassador, Camille tours the world encouraging people to drink French, more specifically, St Germain.

CHRIS HYSTED-ADAMS

Chris Hysted-Adams is one of Australia's most awarded bartenders, and has been a leader of the team at Melbourne's iconic Black Pearl for the best part of a decade. He firmly believes you don't have to take yourself seriously to make seriously good drinks.

EDWARD QUATERMASS

Edward Quatermass is a Brisbane-born bartender who currently runs Maker in South Brisbane. He is passionate about Australian produce and tropical fruits.

HUGH LEECH

Hugh earned his stripes bartending for four years at Gin Palace, one of Melbourne's great cocktail institutions, mixing Martinis and creating cocktails from sundown to sun-up. Developing a love of gin, vermouth, botanical alcohols and making ingredients, he now works at The Bitters Lab, surrounded by bitters, vermouths and amari, as well as assisting with production at Maidenii and the Melbourne Gin Company. He is also a partner in the newly-launched Australian liqueurs company, Marionette Liqueur.

JAMES CONNOLLY

Born and raised in England, James has been living in Perth for over 10 years. He is the beverage manager for Long Chim Group and he likes vermouth (obviously), sandy beaches (plenty of those in WA), gin, tequila and mezcal piña coladas, but nothing beats an ice-cold tinnie of beer!

JOEY JONES

Joe Jones is a bartender, restaurateur and consultant currently operating in Melbourne. With a focus on stripped-back, classic American techniques, his often Euro-centric offerings can be found principally at Romeo Lane (*The Age Good Food Guide*'s Bar of The Year 2016; *Time Out*'s Cocktail Bar of The Year 2017 and Bartender of The Year 2017) and his newly-opened bar and restaurant in Melbourne, The Mayfair.

LOUDON COOPER

Loudon Cooper is a bartender and hospitality professional based in Castlemaine, Victoria. He started off working in local pubs before moving to restaurants, starting at The Good Table then running open-air cocktail bar, Hickster. You can now find him at Bistor Lola, an historic Theatre Royal in Castlemaine, where he is the FOH manager.

MARK WARD

Ex-bartender turned vermouth-maker, Mark is the man behind Australian vermouth brand Regal Rogue.

MICHAEL CHIEM

Michael Chiem is co-owner and bartender at PS40, part world-first cocktail bar, part soda production company in the heart of Sydney's CBD. PS Soda launched commercially in 2017. Their sodas are inspired by cocktails and native Australian ingredients, and they use fresh produce and no preservatives. Michael was awarded Bartender of the Year in 2016 by *Australian Bartender* magazine, and PS40 won *Time Out*'s 2017

Best New Bar and *Australian Bartender*'s 2017 Best Cocktail List and Best Cocktail Bar in NSW, 2017.

SAM CURTIS

Sam has been bartending for 15 years and has a passion for cocktails. He loves left-field flavour combinations and working with colleagues to create new ideas. Hailing from the UK, he now calls Australia, and especially Byron Bay, home.

SAMUEL NG

Sam started his bartending career working in various bars around Melbourne, and eventually became an integral part of the venerable Black Pearl cocktail bar. He also did a short stint at Employee Only in New York prior to that. He currently works for Four Pillars Gin as their Asia Pacific gin ambassador.

SEBASTIAN COSTELLO

Sebastian Costello has been a bartender for just on 18 years. He has visited over 50 distilleries and a large number of wineries. He loves all things booze. Seb has spent the last four years owning and operating Australia's first all-Australian spirit and jaffle bar, Bad Frankie in Melbourne's Fitzroy.

SEBASTIAN RAEBURN

Seb has spent his entire working life in the liquor industry. Behind the bar, Seb opened 1806, which won Best Cocktail List in the World; created the cocktail program at Lui Bar at Vue de Monde, which won Best Restaurant Bar, and co-created Heartbreaker, winner of Best Party Bar, Best Bartender Bar and *The Age Good Food Guide*'s Bar of the Year. In front of the bar, he helped to launch 42 Below in Australia, bring 666 Pure Tasmanian Vodka to life and has spent time pretending to be a corporate manager with Bacardi Martini Australia. He is the house distiller at The Craft & Co and one half of Anther Spirits, which he started with distilling partner, Dr Dervilla McGowan, to create delicious Australian gin.

SEBASTIEN DERBOMEZ

Sebastien is not only Brand Ambassador for Monkey Shoulder in the US, but he is also a celebrated bartender in his own right. Seb has won several awards for outstanding cocktails, service and leadership, including two Australian Bar Awards and a Queensland Lifestyle Award. When Seb is not making cocktails or travelling

the world to discover new cultures and snowboarding, he can be found in New York. He is also a wine lover and is obsessed with cooking and mixing flavours.

TRISH BREW

The most affable and charming Trish Brew currently holds up the Gin Palace bar in Melbourne. She won *Time Out*'s Bartender of the Year 2018.

THE SOMMELIERS

ALEXANDRE JEAN

Based in Paris, Alexandre Jean has been a sommelier many years, working at such prestigious establishments as LA Tour d'Argent, Lucas Carton and Astrance before developing his own consultancy, in particular with La Condesa.

MARK REGINATO

Born and bred in Adelaide, Mark Reginato travelled the world in managerial positions in the hospitality industry, particular in the UK, before he established his own well-respected distribution companies: Connect Vines and Man of Spirit.

NICOLA MUNARI, MD OF TAILLEVANT, LONDON

Born in Piedmont, Nicola Munari has worked in the wine and drink industry on various projects in Asia, Australia, New Zealand, France and the UK. Based in Paris, he has recently joined La Vinicole, the distribution branch of the well-established Moueix family.

RAUL MORENO YAGUE, SOMELLIER AT TIPO 00

Originally from Seville in Spain, Raul Moreno Yague is a sherry educator, sommelier and winemaker in various countries, and will never confirm nor deny rumours that he once attended a Spanish bullfighting school. Raul won the 2018 *Good Food Guide*'s Sommelier of the Year.

REBECCA LINES, BANKSII, SYDNEY

Bec met Hamish in 2009 while working at Billy Kwong. She never expected they'd own their first restaurant, Bar H, together by 2010. In 2012, Rebecca was a finalist in the Electrolux Appetite for Excellence Young Restaurateur of the Year award and, in 2013, both

Hamish and Rebecca consulted for The Four Seasons Hotel on the opening of restaurant, The Woods, and bar, Grain Bar. Her love for boutique vermouth led to the opening of Banksii Vermouth Bar & Bistro, the first vermouth restaurant and bar in Australia.

THE CHEFS

BEN SHEWRY, ATTICA, MELBOURNE

Born and raised in rural North Taranaki on the rugged West Coast of New Zealand's North Island, Ben Shewry is the chef and owner of the internationally-acclaimed Attica restaurant in Melbourne. Ben is a leading advocate for responsible and sustainable eating and cooking in restaurants, as well as being the proud father of three.

HAMISH INGHAM, BANKSII, SYDNEY

Hamish has been a quiet achiever in the Sydney restaurant scene since he became Head Chef at Billy Kwong in 2000. In 2004, he won the prestigious Josephine Pignolet Young Chef of the Year award and headed to the US where he worked at Gramercy Tavern, Craft and Amy's Bakery in New York before heading to San Francisco to work at Alice Water's seminal Chez Panisse. A dish cooked by Hamish is always generous and honest. He is unafraid of flavour and is often bold in its application, however lightness, harmony and balance are the hallmarks of an 'Ingham' dish.

INDRA CARRILLO, LA CONDESA, PARIS

At 29 years of age, Mexican chef Indra Carillo opened his first restaurant in 2017 in Paris. With his gold-plated CV and multi-influence cooking, he has already attracted much acclaim from gastronomic critics.

KYLIE KWONG, BILLY KWONG, SYDNEY

Kylie Kwong has become synonymous with modern Chinese cooking in Australia. As a third-generation Australian, she has drawn on her southern Chinese heritage to reinterpret Cantonese cuisine, combining uniquely Australian ingredients with traditional Chinese cooking methods and flavours at her celebrated eating house Billy Kwong in Sydney. The foundation of her food is locally-grown, organic and biodynamic produce, with a strong focus on native Australian ingredients.

OTHERS

CAMERON MACKENZIE, DISTILLER

Before throwing his lot into the production of craft spirits, Cameron was a fifteen-year veteran of the wine industry, having made, sold, marketed and judged many of Victoria's best-known wine brands, including Yarra Ridge, St Huberts, Punt Road, Sutton Grange, Innocent Bystander/Giant Steps and Rob Dolan Wines. Cameron is the distiller, founding partner, operations guru, educator, locavore, marmalade-chef-bottling-line superintendent, still shiner and despatch director. He is, quite simply, the heart and soul of Four Pillars. Cameron has used his intuitive understanding of flavour and balance to become a real expert at the craft of distillation, and his love for Wilma the still, named after his late mother, knows virtually no bounds.

MAX ALLEN, WINE JOURNALIST

Max Allen is an award-winning wine journalist and author. He is currently working on his next book: a history of drinking in Australia.

ABOUT THE AUTHORS

GILLES LAPALUS

With over 30 years experience in the industry, Gilles Lapalus has wine flowing through his veins. The third generation of a wine-producing family hailing from the Cluny region of Burgundy, Gilles embarked on a prestigious career that has seen him work as a winemaker in the French regions of Burgundy, Languedoc, Medoc, and Beaujolais, and further afield in Tuscany, Campania, Chile and Australia. As an educator, Gilles was part of the Institut Français du Gout, developing taste education in France. In 2001, Gilles moved to Australia to become the manager of biodynamic viticulture and winemaking at Sutton Grange Winery near Castlemaine, Victoria. He first experimented with botanicals in 2011 and, after meeting Shaun, Gilles became a co-founder of Maidenii vermouth. In 2009, while developing Maidenii, Gilles launched his own wine company, Maison LAPALUS with wine production under the Bertrand Bespoke label.

SHAUN BYRNE

Shaun has been mixing drinks since he was legally allowed to do so and hasn't really stopped! After spending four years in the UK working in both restaurants and bars, he returned to Australia to become part of the Gin Palace family. He remained there for eight years, during which time he, along with Gilles, started Maidenii. He also completed a degree in entrepreneurship, launched his consulting company, Good Measure, and met his wife-to-be, Ellen. After leaving Gin Palace, Shaun started another new company called Marionette, a liqueur company working directly with Australian farmers to produce cocktail staple liqueurs. What is next on the cards for Shaun? Well, aside from his wife saying 'no more new businesses!' you can be sure he'll never be too far from the drinks industry, in one form or another.

BIBLIOGRAPHY

Banks, Leigh and Nargess, *The Life Negroni*, Spinach Publishing, 2015.

Brickell, Christopher (ed.) *Encyclopedia of Plants & Flowers*, Dorling Kindersley, 2010.

Brown, Deni, *Encyclopedia of Herbs*, Dorling Kindersley, 2008.

Brown, Jared and Anistatia Miller, *The Mixellany Guide to Vermouth and Other Apéritifs*, Mixellany, 2011.

Craddock, Harry, *The Savoy Cocktail Book*, Pavilion, 2011.

DeGroff, Dale, *The Essential Cocktail*, Clarkson Potter, 2008.

Difford, Simon, *Gin: The Bartender's Bible*, Firefly Books, 2013.

Ford, Adam, *Vermouth: The Revival of the Spirit that Created America's Cocktail Culture*, Countryman Press, 2015.

Garrier, Gilbert, *Histoire Sociale et Culturelle du Vin*, Larousse, 1998.

Harrison, Lorraine, *RHS Latin for Gardeners*, Mitchell Beazley, 2012.

Laws, Bill, *Fifty Plants that Changed the Course of History*, David and Charles, 2010.

Lewis, William, *An Experimental History of the Materia Medica*, Johnson, 1791.

Low, Tim, *Wild Food Plants of Australia*, Angus & Robertson, 1991.

MacElhone, Harry, *Harry's ABC of Mixing Cocktails*, Souvenir Press, 2010.

Maiden, Joseph Henry, *The Useful Native Plants of Australia*, Turner and Henderson, 1889.

Mayall, Jude, *The Outback Chef*, New Holland, 2014.

McGovern, Patrick, *Ancient Wine: The Search for the Origins of Viniculture*, Princeton University Press, 2003.

McGovern , Patrick, *Uncorking the Past: The Quest for Wine, Beer, and Other Alcoholic Beverages*, Berkeley University of California, 2009.

Miller, Anistatia and Jared Brown, *Shaken Not Stirred: A Celebration of the Martini*, William Morrow Paperbacks, 2013.

Montanari, Massimo and Jean-Louis Flandrin, *Histoire de L'alimentation*, Fayard, 1996.

Monti, François, *El Gran Libro del Vermut*, Ediciones B , 2015.

Morgenthaler, Jeffrey, *The Bar Book: Elements of Cocktail Technique*, Chronicle Books, 2014.

Newton, John, *The Oldest Foods on Earth*, NewSouth Publishing, 2016.

Page, Karen and Andrew Dornenburg, *The Flavor Bible*, Little Brown and Company, 2008.

Parsons, Brad Thomas, *Amaro: The Spirited World of Bittersweet, Herbal Liqueurs*, Ten Speed Press, 2016.

Rare Vermouth Greats, 5Star Cooks, 2017.

Regan, Garry, *The Negroni: A Gaz Regan Notion*, Mixellany, 2013.

Robinson, Jancis, *Le Livre des Cépages*, Hachette, 1986.

Robinson, Jancis, Julia Harding and José Vouillamoz, *Wine Grapes: A Complete Guide to 1,368 Vine Varieties, including their Origins and Flavours*, Allen Lane, 2012.

Stewart, Amy, *The Drunken Botanist*, Algonquin Books of Chapel Hill, 2013.

Tanner, Hans and Rudolf Brunner, *La distillation moderne des fruits*, Editions Heller, 1982.

Willis, Kathy and Carolyn Fry, *Plants: From Roots to Riches*, John Murray, 2014.

Wittels, Betina J. and Robert Hermesch, *Absinthe, Sip of Seduction: A Contemporary Guide*, Revised Edition, ed. T.A. Breaux, Speck Press, 2008.

Wondrich, David, *Punch*, Perigee, 2010.

www.eur-lex.europa.eu

www.oiv.int

www.penn.museum

www.vermouth101.com

ACKNOWLEDGEMENTS

SHAUN BYRNE

I would like to thank my wife Ellen, who has put up with the hundreds of bottles of liquor strewn throughout our house during the testing and drinking of cocktails that was required to write this book. Thank you darling, you have been a great support during this process.

Both Nick Tesar and Hugh Leech were integral to the production of this book, lending a helping hand and their palates to mix and taste cocktails. The book couldn't have been produced without them, so thank you.

To all of our contributors, thank you for sharing your wonderful recipes and knowledge for this book. Our thanks go to Cameron MacKenzie for his words around juniper (and making great gin, of course!)

Thank you to the team at Hardie Grant, who made this book possible, and to Andrea O'Connor, our patient editor who turned our jumbled words into something coherent. To Jack Hawkins, the amazing photographer with liquor running through his lens, thank you.

Finally, to all the vermouth lovers out there, be it producers, mixers or drinkers, thank you for taking delight in the drink that we love.

GILLES LAPALUS

This book was born when Shaun and I approached Jane Willson at Hardie Grant about translating François Monti's *El Gran Libro del Vermouth* into English. Her enthusiasm on the subject resulted in us writing a book ourselves for the new generation of vermouth drinkers.

Many thanks go to my family on both sides of the equator for my life of good food and great drinks, in particular my partner Jude Anderson, who was the first reader and taster on my vermouth adventure, thank you.

Thank you to Jude Mayall, the passionate supplier of native botanicals, and to Tim Entwisle, at the Royal Botanic Gardens Victoria, for his great support in programming our Boozy Botanicals tour and being an expert contributor of botanical insights. Special thanks to Max Allen for embracing the new movement around vermouth and for his contribution to this book. Thanks as well to Mike Bennie, a great supporter of artisanal wines and spirits.

A big thank you to Vernon Chalker, who was the catalyst for what is now Maidenii vermouth. And Jean Michel, who was at the first session creating Maidenii with Shaun. Also to Ben Shewry and Banjo Harris Plane, who were the first true believers in our first vermouth back in 2012.

Huge thanks to Lauren Bonkowski, the brand designer and design mind behind the Maidenii label and this book. A big thank you to all the chefs, bartenders and other contributors to this book.

Many thanks to the suppliers of our foraged botanicals, wormwood in particular: Genevieve, Martine, Tara, Frank and Melissa, Rosa and Collin and Andre. And thanks to our grape growers, Ian, Stuart, David, Ramon and Steve.

Especially, thank you to all the distinguished drinkers of Maidenii vermouth, be they at bars or restaurants, or simply at home with friends and family.

The publisher would like to thank The Mayfair bar in Melbourne for providing a beautiful space for us to shoot this book.

INDEX

INDEX

INDEX

Published in 2018 by Hardie Grant Books,
an imprint of Hardie Grant Publishing

Hardie Grant Books (Melbourne)
Building 1, 658 Church Street
Richmond, Victoria 3121

Hardie Grant Books (London)
5th & 6th Floors
52–54 Southwark Street
London SE1 1UN

hardiegrantbooks.com

A catalogue record for this
book is available from the
National Library of Australia

The Book of Vermouth
ISBN 978 1 74379 399 2

10 9 8 7 6 5 4 3 2 1

Publishing Director: Jane Willson
Project Manager & Editor: Andrea O'Connor
Design Manager: Jessica Lowe
Designer: Lauren Bonkowski
Typesetter: Patrick Cannon
Photographer: Jack Hawkins
Stylist: Jessica Lillico
Production Manager: Todd Rechner

Colour reproduction by Splitting Image Colour Studio
Printed in China by Leo Paper Product. LTD

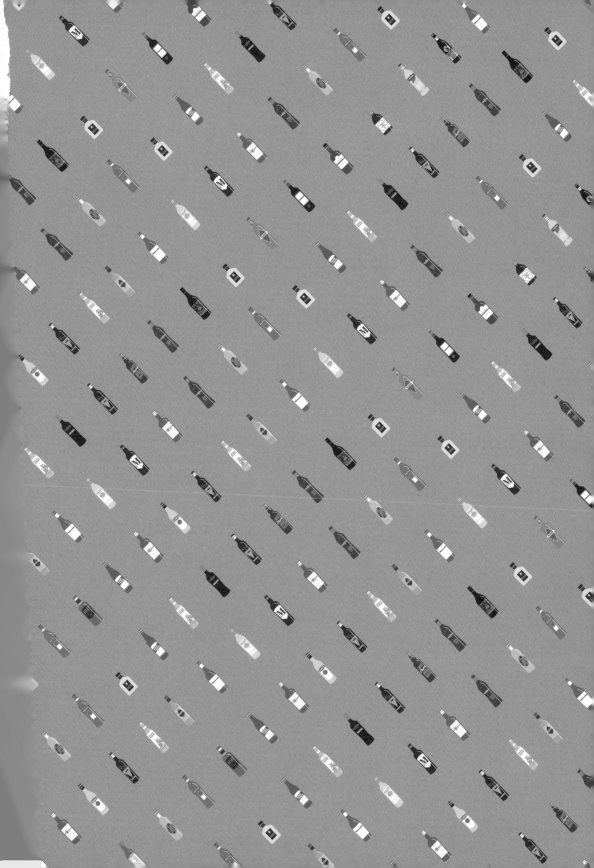

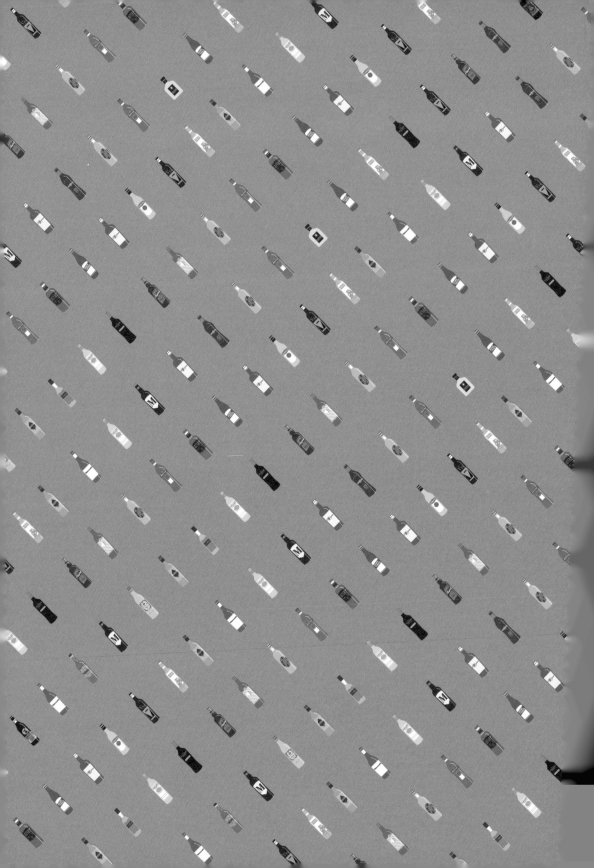